FIND *Her*

20 REVEALING QUESTIONS TO DISCOVER THE WOMAN WITHIN

JANIS DOHERTY

For more information please contact: janis@herwithin.com

First paperback edition September 2020

Revised paperback edition January 2021

Book design by Adam Cullen

Illustrations by JWedholmDesign.ca

Back cover Photographer: My son Taylor

US ISBN 978 1 70284 865 4

www.herwithin.com

CONTENTS

Acknowledgment

Writing a book is harder than I thought and more rewarding than I could have ever imagined. These questions represent the voices of many silent women.

Thank you to my Dream Team of peer editors Josette, Jaime, Jackie, Karen, Kelly, Gail. This book is truly an international labour of love. Your support, suggestions, and edits aligned with every energetic cell in my body.

A special thank you to Leonie Overbeek for her professional editing, guidance and support. Divine timing brought us together and my heart is forever grateful for your presence.

Thank you to my sons Taylor & Adam. My heart is bursting. Mum did it!

Thank you to my husband Paul. Your love and support are the biggest reasons this book got published.

Thank you to all my friends, family and HERwithin followers. To answer your continually supportive question "how's the book coming?" HERE IT IS!

Every accomplishment starts with the decision to try.

- Anonymous

Introduction

Within every woman is something I have named HERwithin. As a little girl you are deeply connected to HER and she may even be your imaginary friend. That connection within is what guides you to your answers, imagination and play. As you grow up, your beliefs and opinions begin to be shaped by those around you. You're influenced by your parents, relatives, teachers, leaders and peers. What happens when our beliefs are being shaped by the world around us? What happens when you spend more time fitting in rather than being accepted for who you are and what you think? You lose your connection to HER. She is that knowing voice within you that guides you through your journey in life. When that connection is lost, you may start having feelings of being unfulfilled, lost or confused. The accumulation of limiting beliefs, self-imposed judgements or outside opinions that change the course of your life path are the internal barriers that break your connection with HER.

The good news is that the internal connection to HER is never completely lost. You've just wandered too far down another path that's adjacent to the one your HERwithin was supposed to walk you down. She's still sending you messages, but you can't hear them or feel them because of those internal barriers. Without the answers that come from within, you may start to find yourself having more questions than answers. Questions that might keep you up at night might be "why do I put up with so much" or "why do I feel like this" or my turning point question, "how did I get here". It's not the questions that are the problem. It's the absence of answers. Have you read a stack of self-help books with no answers? Have you had long conversations with family and friends searching for answers? The answers you're looking for are within you. You and HER hold all your answers and all you have to do is Find HER again.

How do I Find HER? You Find HER when you start removing those internal barriers that brought you here. This book is a "first steps tool" for asking yourself deeper questions that will reveal some of your internal barriers. Each question in the book includes my experiences, wisdom and guidance. I want you to know that you aren't alone on your journey. This is the time in your life when you shine a brighter light on the things that need to be resolved so you can move forward, feeling more fulfilled. Isn't that what life is all about? You want to live a fulfilled life, but you can't when you feel lost and confused.

My journey took a turn in 2016 when my mum passed away. A few months prior to her passing, we had a conversation about regret. I didn't think I had any regrets, but I knew as I watched her body fail, I didn't want to have the same conversation with my family. The day after her birthday and the day before she passed, I sat by a river and felt completely lost and confused. I wasn't enjoying my job; I was cranky at home and I didn't like how I felt. I needed to find those elusive answers, but I had no idea where they were. My first step was leaving my job and searching for something that would help me find my answers. That ended up being a retreat in California, where I spent 3 days learning how to reconnect with my body. Movement, mantra and meditation brought a sensation to my body that was so foreign to me. This sparked something within me that brought the awareness that there is something within me that I was disconnected from. It was HER and I was on a mission to Find HER again.

The next three years were spent learning about myself through meditation, coaches, journaling and a lot of vulnerability. That hard exterior I was hiding behind was softening and the authentic Janis was shining through. I was speaking at women's events, hosted a podcast, offering mentorship through the HERwithin online community and sharing my wisdom like candy on Halloween. Then in May 2019, I was diagnosed with breast cancer. This life-changing event put me and HER to the test. With 2 surgeries, recovery, radiation, and more recovery, you can imagine the amount of time I had to think and process. I was going into this next stage of my journey with HER by my side. I understood my energy in a new way that allowed me to process emotions that found space to bubble up. I understood expectations, boundaries, trust and stillness in ways I had never experienced before. I had space and grace to heal, process and release and each night my gratitude list grew and grew because I allowed myself to receive and love. All because I took the time to Find HER.

When you allow yourself to step into the unknown and let your guard down, you will find beauty in everything you do. Being vulnerable is a beautiful thing. There's no need to be on guard any longer when you Find HER. There is no judgement from within. Everything that comes your way comes with Love. The judgement you hear and feel is Ego. Its job is to protect you using fear, so you don't hurt yourself. Stepping into the unknown with HER can be scary if you let Ego take the wheel. Take the step forward and know that you've got this. Your HERwithin is you. You know what to do intuitively. It's those internal barriers that create the fear. It's time to let down your guard, drop your armour and start asking yourself those deeper questions that will reveal your answers.

I promise if you read this book with the intention to understand internal barriers, find answers and Find HER, you will do exactly that. When you show up, do the journaling right after you read a question, you will receive answers, relief, and maybe more questions. These questions are meant to get your internal energy flowing again. I can't promise you won't cry when you feel something trigger you. If that happens, get to the journal page and start writing. Those emotions are Energy in Motion. They want out, so let them out. The more you process, the more you'll peel away. There are women around the world walking the wrong path and they don't know there's another path to follow. Are you on YOUR path?

The longer you wait to start making changes in your life, more layers build up. A lady in her seventies came up to me after a talk and said, "Where were you twenty years ago? You could have saved me a lot of time." I am saving YOU a lot of time by sharing the questions I asked myself. All the questions in this book came to me one afternoon when I was sitting by a river. There's something very therapeutic about flowing water. I couldn't stop the questions. It was like I was writing a final exam on ME! That entire impromptu afternoon of writing happened because I listened to HER when I got a nudge to take a journal and go for a drive to 'the river'. I don't question HER any longer. If I did, I probably wouldn't be writing this book and changing lives around the world.

Start asking yourself questions that will start revealing your internal landscape. Nobody can fix your self-limiting beliefs but you. Yes, it's ugly work but look at it this way... If your computer has a virus and it kept glitching when you did a certain task, would you leave the virus in there? Probably not. When you leave a virus (negative energy) in something, it grows and causes bigger problems. The same goes for self-limiting beliefs. Ignore it, and it will surface again without warning. Suppress it and it will start manifesting into an ailment that you don't want. Face it, remove it and you'll go through the rest of your life without that fear of being triggered by that "virus" again.

- Excerpt from Question #1 - Am I taking responsibility for my experiences?

When you gather allies to
make yourself feel better, it
only makes you a victim.

QUESTION #1

Am I taking responsibility for my experiences?

I remember my mum always had a comic strip from Family Circus taped inside a cupboard door. Every time I think of it now, I giggle at "Ida Know and Not Me" who were the funny little characters that created the havoc in the comic strip. How many of us still do that? We blame someone else for what's going on. I know when I was younger, I didn't take responsibility for my experiences and pointed the finger at anyone who would cross my path.

It's much easier for us not to take responsibility for our experiences and then wait and watch as related issues start to bubble up. When you're involved in conflict, if each person took responsibility for their part in that conflict, imagine how fast things could be resolved? How many lingering issues do you have in your life that could be resolved if you take responsibility for your actions and experiences? All it takes is for one person to do it and half the issue is resolved. I was faced with this twice within a month and realized that regardless of how I took responsibility for what I did, or didn't do, other people may not be satisfied because of an unmet expectation they had. It's probably time for them to take responsibility for their expectations. More on that in Question #7.

When you're faced with shadows that bubble up from your past, it means that you can observe the experiences with greater clarity & recognize that you haven't taken responsibility for your part in that experience. Habitual reactions can be a leading cause of conflict. These are those phrases or comments that just jump out as a reaction rather than a thoughtful response. Those can be resolved instantly by taking responsibility for what was just said. It's as simple as a do-over, or mulligan. You're human, you make mistakes and learning how to fix them right away shows that you are taking responsibility for your experiences. Little conversation fixes are the stepping stones to the bigger character issues that are part of your DNA. When I hear people say things like, "my family doesn't apologize to each other", that's a danger sign. If you don't take responsibility for what you say, do or feel with your family, you allow for that experience to leak out into the world like a virus. Work on the experiences that are closest to your heart and then expand out from there.

I just went through this in my family. Since our mum's passing in 2016, I had contact with one of my brothers about five times. I said something that he took offense to. I apologized over the years, but nothing was going to change how he took whatever I said. He came to a family birthday party three years later and I stood up, walked over to him and gave him a big hug. We both teared up for a few moments and the door to healing opened. No judgement, no "you should have", simply a bond between a brother and sister. I took responsibility and laid down my hammer.

Take the time to recognize where you may not be facing your responsibilities with others, and especially with yourself. What are you doing to yourself that's causing pain or affecting your ability to succeed? When I realized that my internal dialogue was tainted, I took it upon myself to fix it, and clean up the negative self-talk that was stopping my personal growth. When you take responsibility for your experiences and your interactions with the world around you, everything becomes lighter and easier to process.

I had a coach tell me that I take responsibility for my experiences as we were uncovering some false beliefs about myself. I wasn't sure what to make of that statement. Then she explained to me that I call myself out when I understand why I'm holding back or making excuses. That's not something I would have voluntarily done in the past. When your finger turns and points back at you, self-discovery work is well underway. If you're still blaming others for your experiences, it's time to stop. Graciously ask others to grant you a do-over so you can revisit the situation and then ask yourself some deep questions. Start with "why am I being triggered by this and avoiding taking responsibility?" Chances are you won't find the answer right away because your ego will be standing guard. Its instant response is, "not my fault" and places you into protective custody so you're safe from moving into a state of feeling unguarded or vulnerable. Your ego does not like change. If you've always done things a certain way, be prepared for your ego to start sending you a rapid-fire string of excuses and finger-pointing when you begin shifting your ways.

My biggest experience with taking responsibility was with my stepdaughter. I found myself being the victim of many circumstances which, I later found out, I was the root cause of. I discovered that I had been carrying around a self-limiting belief that I needed to face. Avoidance of the situation wasn't working. From each character that appears on my life stage I have something to learn. I'm only realizing this now. My stepdaughter wasn't doing anything wrong; she was triggering something within me that I needed to face. Does this make sense? Have you heard people say that you will keep experiencing the same thing over and over until you learn your lesson from it? That's what was happening here. I had a self-limiting belief that I wasn't important. I talk more about that in Question #9. Each time I was in a situation where attention was shifted to her, my ego jumped into gear and started reminding me, at a conscious level, that I wasn't important. As soon as I realized that was happening, I completely understood, and I could feel the energy in my body shifting gears back down.

This insight and new way of being doesn't happen overnight. There's a period of adjustment that I needed so that, if I feel triggered, I needed to realize why. When you're truly past something, there's no longer a trigger. The hard part is convincing others that I've changed. When there's been years of me behaving a certain way, others develop a trigger as well. The way I act is changing because I'm taking responsibility for my experiences. I can't be responsible for the experience of others. If someone is still triggered by the chance that I might be triggered, evidence is confidence. When I display non-triggering behaviour, they will have the evidence, which will create the confidence that all is well. Don't forget that they too need to deal with the situation within themselves. Why are they triggered by this?

Apply this to any situation where you feel anxious, sad, angry, dismissed, nervous or even belittled. When that energetic shift happens within you, it's time to read deeper into what's going on so you can take responsibility. When something triggers you, it's a sign that you have some work to do. Nobody can fix your self-limiting beliefs but you. Yes, it's ugly work but look at it this way... If your computer has a virus and it kept glitching when you did a certain task, would you leave the virus in there? Probably not. When you leave a virus (negative energy) in something, it grows and causes bigger problems. Much like self-limiting beliefs. Ignore it, and it will surface again without warning. Suppress it and it will start manifesting into an ailment that you don't want. Face it, remove it and you'll go through the rest of your life without that fear of being triggered by that "virus" again.

What do you need to take responsibility for? You might not even know what the problem is, but you may be aware of what kinds of situations trigger an energetic shift in your body. Take time to write them down, name them and work on discovering their roots. An energetic healer can help you pull things through your energetic and nervous system to help release them. Taking responsibility for your experiences is a beautiful step to help your energy flow with ease and grace.

FINDING *Her*
NEXT STEPS

1. Identify your triggers. In order to take responsibility for your experiences, you need to identify the experiences that cause you to shift internally. Write them down when they happen and be honest with yourself. Use "I" statements rather than "they did this" or "she said that". Speak to yourself in your writing. Use the journal section of the book or a journal or even your phone if it's handy in the moment. Once you identify, your awareness will start to change rapidly, and you will see how to take responsibility rather than blaming others.

2. What's your internal dialogue? What's the story that you're telling yourself while something is happening or even after the fact. You know that story that keeps repeating itself in your head long after it has happened? That's the internal dialogue you want to become aware of. You know it's happening so start writing it down. Are you blaming others? Are you self-deprecating yourself? Are you giving it the "whatever" so it goes away? News Flash... it doesn't go away until you face the reality of why it's happening.

3. What self-limiting beliefs are you carrying around? There's something stopping you from taking responsibility for your experiences and once you find the root, your actions and reactions will start to make more sense. There are many steps to uncovering answers, but the good news is, the answers are all within you. Write things down or

record them in some way. Talk to family members that may remember things from your past. It's time to become a detective in your own life. The answers are in there for you to find.

What bubbled up?

What bubbled up?

When you receive, you give
someone the gift of joy.

QUESTION #2

Am I giving more than I'm receiving?

Women are natural givers. We help, nurture, guide and give. If someone needs help, I offer my services. If a child is struggling with something, I jump in to help. Some women are over-givers, and you see them always doing for others. You may even praise them for their acts of kindness. In return, they can also be the ones who don't believe they deserve to have anything done for them. "I'm fine, that's ok." is their tribal call. I know this because I was an over-giver. Doing for others and giving felt great and filled my heart with pride when I made another person happy. The question is, why did I have a need to give so much?

When you give to fill a void within yourself, many times you don't understand why. It's not until you start peeling back layers and digging deeper that the truth is revealed. It could be from a need to be acknowledged or hear praise or even just receive attention. Whatever the void is, over-giving of yourself isn't going to fix it. The void needs to be filled from within once it's recognized.

My void was the need to be appreciated and wanted. I was highly involved with my two sons, driving around sports teams, organizing events, hosting parties, volunteering, and the list goes on. There was a void I was filling by giving of myself and my time. It wasn't until 2016 that I started to understand how I justified what I did and why I did it. When you don't receive what you need, you instinctively seek it externally. For me, it was giving. When I give, I make people happy which in turn made me happier. At least for a bit. It was the equivalent of a 3pm chocolate bar, and the internal gratification always wore off. So, I'd do it again. Sounds like an addiction doesn't it? Not far off. When the buzz was gone, I needed to find another source to fill my void.

Here's the downside of being so generous with time and offerings. When you over-give, you're setting up an expectation that you will always do it. You know the saying, "ask the busiest person to do something and they'll get it done". Then comes the day when you don't, and all hell breaks loose. When you have a pattern of over-giving, it can turn into resentment when it starts to feel like a one-way street. That's when it's time to set up some boundaries for yourself. I faced this when someone expected me to show up the way I'd always done in the past. My transitional journey taught me to establish boundaries and stop overstepping my line. I didn't need to fill an internal void any longer with acknowledgments from others. I was filling it from within.

Now's the time for me to start receiving. When I was in my go-go mode of giving, I never needed anything from anyone. It wasn't until someone said to me once, "when you deny me the opportunity to give to you, you're denying me that feeling you have when you give". That opened my eyes to understand that although it was uncomfortable for me to receive, I was still giving by allowing the other person to experience the joy of giving. I can happily say that I no longer have issues receiving gifts in many forms. Anything from praise to a Green Tea Latte fills my heart. Something as simple as a handshake is the process of giving and receiving. You each offer your hand (giving), you shake the others' hand (giving) and you're getting a handshake in return (receiving).

Let me warn you about an adjustment period and a tendency to create a backdraft of receiving. As a recovering "giver", I know how hard it is to be on the receiving end with intention. "No, I'm good, thanks." could be heard from me daily. But you know what? Once I said it, I would turn on myself internally. You see, my HERwithin knew that I wanted whatever was being offered. My ego told me that I wasn't worthy of having it based on my beliefs. Beliefs are like a deeply worn path that runs in our minds. The grooves are so deep because we've been doing and saying the same things for years. Have you ever been to a party and the hosts asks you if you'd like something to drink? If you're like me, the old me, "I'll just have a glass of water.", would be the acceptable response according to my ego. Then you look around the room and see how many people are drinking wine or cocktails. Queue the internal judgement team. See the cycle that happens?

When you deny yourself the things you crave or desire, that's a direct indication that you are not connected to your HERwithin. I'm not saying she wants wine, but she knows what you want. Your inner critic is working off old patterns that you've surrendered to and don't have to think about. It just happens. But what happens when you disrupt those old patterns? That's when a part of your subconscious flips out and puts you into protective custody. Martha Beck, best-selling author, life coach, and speaker, calls it your inner lizard. Imagine you're about to make a big decision. Your heart is pounding and you take the first step. Then all of a sudden, you're questioning your ability to make this change. That red flag is your inner lizard. Your ego is programmed to protect you. When change happens and you're resistant to it, your subconscious is basically sending you a warning signal...

"YOU'RE GONNA DIE!! DON'T DO IT!!" It wants things to stay the same. That's why you stay in these habits of being a giver and unable to receive because that's just the way you're programmed. You have the power to change that. It might be uncomfortable but it's a lot easier than you think. Allow yourself to receive. If someone offers to buy you a coffee, receive it with a "thank you, that would be nice." Then take a moment to feel that gratitude. I guarantee your inner lizard is going to jump up and start throwing stuff at you like, "why are they offering to buy? What do they want?" But remember, when someone offers to take your kids or look after an ailing relative, receive it with grace and a thank you. Everyone benefits from giving and receiving when it's a two-way street.

My receiving awakening happened with my second marriage. I had no problem receiving gifts at Christmas, my birthday or Valentines Day. My problem arose when he wanted to buy me a latte at Starbucks, or a meal or simply pay for something when we were both out shopping. Inside, I needed to look after myself. I couldn't allow anyone to do something like that for me. I had justified it with the fact that I had my own money, he had two kids still living at home and damn it, I can look after myself! What was happening is that whenever I was in a "who pays" situation, I jumped into action to take over and pay. I didn't offer, I just took over and I was putting a strain on our relationship. He wanted to pay and I was taking the love out of it. What was I doing? I was doing everything but swatting his wallet out of his hand. In his mind, that's what my actions symbolized. In my mind, if I let him pay, it set off warning bells that I owed him something in return, which I didn't. I had the internal judgement gallery chiming in telling me that I wasn't independent enough to look after myself. I now know that what I was feeling, was fear and a gigantic energy shift into … CONTROL! If I'm in control, I don't have to trust. (Question 12 covers this in more detail). How unnatural is that?

I trust my husband to my core, yet when my husband wanted to buy me dinner, I struggled with an internal battle. Interestingly, we came to an agreement for a while where whoever suggested we go out, pays. That way there was no question and my energy army could be at ease. Now, I have zero issues with being treated to dinners, lunches, flowers, coffee or gifts from my husband. I, in turn, treat him because he deserves my love in whatever love language I speak. By refusing his gifts, I was refusing his love. If you're familiar with the 5 Languages of Love by Gary Chapman, we all express love in our own way. Words of Affirmation, Acts of Service, Receiving Gifts, Quality Time, and Physical Touch. I highly recommend doing the online quiz to find out what Language of Love you speak because you'll understand yourself and everyone around you in a new way.

My over-giving days are done. I used to drop and run to be a rescuer whenever I could because of that void that needed filling. Now that void is filled with a beautiful light from within. It's my source. I know where to find that light and I know what to do to fill myself up. If I'm lacking in love, I can't expect to receive it from others. It's not their job to fill my void. The next time you find yourself in a position to give, ask yourself if you're giving more than you're receiving. If the answer is yes, it's time to set some boundaries and re-establish your self-worth because you are worthy of receiving. That void you're trying to fill can be filled from within. Follow the path to your heart and you'll see a little sign that says "start here".

FINDING *Her*
NEXT STEPS

1. How are you programmed? Look at the people in your life that influenced your behaviours. What did you see happening with your mom, aunts, grandmothers, sisters, etc. What you see and what you're taught when you're younger is what sets the stage for your behaviours. Remember that you're also cellularly connected to your birth mother. That stuff was implanted in you before birth. Take the time to look at your lineage and see what behaviours are not aligned with you any longer. Write them down, make a spreadsheet, record voice messages to yourself. You need to create an awareness which may create a trigger when you see it happening, but you'll know how to work through that too.

2. Patterns of over giving need to be faced and understood. Where are you doing it? Who are you doing it with? Why are you doing it? Become aware of the who, what, where, when and why's of your giving patterns. More recording is needed until you see the patterns. Remember, those triggers that come up are there for you to face and resolve so you can move forward with success. Receiving with grace is going to be a tough one to do if it's not in your DNA.

3. You need to become aware of every time you say "no thanks, I'm good" or anything that sounds like that. Someone offers to buy you a coffee, your homework is to

say, "thank you, that would be nice" and do everything in your power to smile and receive it with grace. Remember, when you deny someone the gift of giving you something or doing something for you, you're taking away the joy that you feel when you do the same for someone else. When you receive, you give someone the gift of joy.

Thoughts & Feelings

Thoughts & Feelings

We're changing together

because of something new.

QUESTION #3

Am I expecting others to change for me?

This transition journey I've been going through, as I mentioned in the introduction, has me changing with every moment of awareness. Before I started understanding the emotional body and the connection between mind, body and soul, I was working against myself. I was completely aware of the changes I was going through in the beginning. It was mainly about trust and boundaries. I set a boundary, and the people I would allow across it, were met with a new Janis. I wasn't allowing the same behaviours to continue. Being new to all this change and new versions of myself, I was essentially expecting others to change, in order to honour those boundaries that I had worked hard to establish and enforce. It's not about expecting others to change FOR you, it's about them changing WITH you. We're changing together because of something new. I don't expect anyone to change for me. When I put in the work and it's something that I believe in, then we change our path together and nobody is forcing the other to do anything. For those who choose to set up camp in the past and not keep up with the changes, I can't dishonour the work I've done on myself and issue them a special pass for boundary jumping. If my change is triggering something within them, that's for them to dig deeper into. Maybe share Question #7 with them. I've aligned myself to what feels energetically right for me.

We wear masks when we want to fit in. I can't do that any

longer. I need to be accepted for who I am and the free spirit I can connect to within me. It hurts to be unaligned with who I am now. I bring honesty, love, humour and wisdom to those I connect with. When expectations are put on me to be who I was, and I fail to meet the expectations of others, I have to remind them I've changed and found new ways to move through my journey. It would be unfair of me to expect them to change to meet my needs. Changing to meet the needs of others was the way of our house when I became an official stepmom in 2014. I had a gradual induction into stepparenting for two years before that and I will be the first to admit that I probably wore the step-monster hat numerous times.

I am very proud of my parenting skills, and when I was a stay-at-home mum, I couldn't think of anything more fulfilling in life. After my divorce, nobody took my mum hat away and I still had two amazing sons in their late teens. While raising my sons in my first marriage, I was a master at burying my feelings and pretending everything was ok. My focus was on my sons and I poured all my love into them. Enter my new husband and his family. Take that love of being a mum and drop it into a pre-existing family that has their own mother, and you'd think everything could work out just fine. Unfortunately for me, and eventually everyone else, I didn't realize the amount tightly packed emotional luggage I brought with me.

All of those emotions were about to start unpacking themselves. Everything I needed to work on and everything I was trying to avoid in life started popping up like giant irritating dust bunnies. Because I hadn't faced my emotions in the past, I was carrying them around like my winter sweaters. When we have buried emotions and we find new people in our lives, those people act as a mirror for you to reflect on those buried emotions. I now had four new people in my life that had no idea they were about to help me unpack. My husband and his children, ages 11, 14 and 16 were figuring out their own lives. They had just been through a divorce two years earlier, the kids were learning to move from house to house every week, trying to establish new routines and finding a groove with their dad in a new home. When I entered the scene, I had expectations about how things would work. These were expectations that I brought from my world and thought they would be adapted into this new world of mine because I'm an adult. If I knew then what I know now, I would have taken myself aside and had a serious reality talk with myself.

I was entering this family with control issues, so many expectations on how things should work and how they should change for me. Why? Because I knew what I was doing. I was super mum, and I know how to make a household run smoothly. Insert LOL! Rather pretentious of me, wasn't it? So many stepmoms come into families and bring their baggage with them expecting others to change for them. It's not about anyone changing for anyone. There may be some habits or teaching things that need to happen because of the age of the children, but the reality is that these kids are now on my life stage and the lessons I was about to learn are not for the faint of heart. The things they did that would trigger me were things that I needed to work on. They didn't have to change one bit if it was something that triggered me. They weren't doing anything on purpose. They were bringing awareness to something within me that needed to be tended to in order to release it. Think about it. Who in your life triggers you? What are they doing that's triggering you? What are you feeling? Where have you felt like that before? More about that in Question #8. It might not be what you think, but it's being presented to you to recognize and change. If they feel the need to change, it's because of something you're doing that's triggering them.

To bring expectations into any relationship is a harsh thing to do. As a former control freak, I understand that control was the result of lacking trust. Not just trusting others but trusting myself. If I had control of things, I didn't have to trust others and they wouldn't disappoint me when they didn't do it my way. Expectations are controlling so when we expect others to change for us, we're in fact exhibiting a controlling behaviour. The work that needs to be done is with you. When you become aware of your triggering, dig deep and find that place where it's happened before. Maybe it's even happened before that too. Keep digging. When you make a change within, to honour and trust yourself, people will change and flow with you. When it comes from love, it's accepted by all. When it comes from fear, it's resisted by many. Expectations come from fear. Am I expecting others to change for me now? Absolutely not! It can take a long time for people to accept my new ways as I change. If people know the old you and now, you're acting and responding differently, give them time to experience it, understand it and accept that this is the new you.

FINDING *Her*
NEXT STEPS

1. Control and change are polar opposites and I can tell you from experience that when change is happening, being in control of that change is habitual and you need to step back from it. The change I'm talking about is the change that people are experiencing. They will experience it at their own pace and through their own lens. You can't control that. The only change you can control is your own. Focus on that and just keep giving people positive evidence that you've changed. Stay true to yourself, ask for do-overs if you need them and give everything the time it needs to re-establish itself as the new norm.

2. Let others digest what's going on at their own pace. Your changes will be digested at a different pace based on who they are. The older they are, the longer it will take. The more issues they have, the more you could trigger them. Some men will digest it faster than some women and that's their journey. You can't force feed anyone. People who have experienced your behaviour for many years will say things like, "Well you usually..." or "I was expecting you to...". You need to create a positive response to those statements that will gradually dilute their reactions. It takes time and it's worth every ounce of energy you put into it. Don't react with anger that they don't get it. Sometimes I just raise my eyebrows with a smile and say, "I'm full of surprises, aren't I?" Later I'll have a conversation about my new behaviours

and ask for their support as we move forward.

3. Change is scary and emotions will surface. Be aware that emotions are energy moving through your body. Sometimes you may be making changes and feel tears coming up. Those could be tears of pride or tears of fear. Whatever the emotion is, allow it to move through you. Making changes to your way of being, especially around your fifties, is scary. I know that first hand. Journal or record what's going on. Changes to relationships that don't align with your new way is also normal. Friendships can dissolve and you'll start seeing things through a new lens of clarity. If it feels like it needs to change, don't fight it. Keep track of your energy in situations and with different people. You'll see patterns and clarity.

What did you reveal?

There's power in The Pause

in any conversation.

QUESTION #4

Do I taste my words before I speak them?

How easy is it to react to a text, call or person without putting your words through a filter? It's pretty darn easy to do, but it's also something that you can change with awareness and intention. One of the greatest tips I learned about responding vs reacting was from one of my life coaches. She mentioned that before you respond to someone, ask yourself these three questions; 1) Does this need to be said? 2) Does this need to be said now? 3) Does this need to be said by me? These three questions have stopped me from many habitual reactions rather than responding appropriately. When I ask myself those three questions, and I get a yes from all three, I intentionally taste my words before I speak them. I remove any added spiciness, sour notes, attitude and tone before I proceed. Sometimes when I ask myself those three questions, I forget what I wanted to say and just smile. The benefits of being in my fifties.

You probably know people who have "tone" when they talk. Sometimes it can make you feel belittled or on guard. It feels yucky, doesn't it? How you feel when someone talks to you is the experience you are responsible for. Tone, words, inflections and posture can be energetic triggers for some. Regardless of how something is said or what is said, it can trigger another person because of their personal experiences. If you take the time to make sure you don't say something tainted, then how can you ensure that the other person isn't triggered even after you've processed what you're about to say? You can't. Our experiences in life create our triggers. You can say something with the purest intention and still trigger someone. You can verbally spit fire at someone else and get no reaction whatsoever. It's their journey and responsibility to process your words. It's your responsibility to communicate your thoughts and feelings by responding and not reacting. Do you spew reactions that are programmed within you? When you're faced with the same situation over and over and react, without pausing or processing, that habit is coming from emotion.

This was very apparent one day when I saw some young teenagers vaping inside a fast food restaurant. Right there, in the corner, and we could all see the vape smoke. I took it upon myself to go over and remind them that this is a restaurant and there's no smoking or vaping allowed inside. Guess what the first two words were that came out of the ring leader's mouth? These kids were no older than fourteen, so yes, that's right, F*** YOU. That was a reaction. There wasn't even a split second for him to process what I had said before that came out of his mouth. I'm sure if he could have tasted his words, they would have tasted like shards of glass. I took that moment to return to my seat and continue eating my meal and knew that I had acted responsibly by not reacting to the words. It was a very graceful moment in my life that would have ended differently if I hadn't tasted my words before I spoke, and after as well.

I had another incident where I needed to respond to a text. I had to remove myself from a group text because I was being triggered. I take full ownership of my need to leave the group. I instilled my boundaries after a conversation with myself, and kindly asked to be removed. The other person kindly did that and then followed up with a personal text to me asking if I was offended by anything. The text I wanted to send was all typed out. I was reacting to this person's disregard for my situation. Problem was, they didn't know what my situation was. Yes, I was unfairly about to spit fire at them because of a situation I was having over here in my corner. I think I retyped that extended response three or four times. Then I sat with my phone in my hand, feeling something different. Why was I pausing? Was I questioning my actions? Ironically, this chapter wasn't as long as I wanted it to be. It needed more content, so, I left a note on my computer that said: "Revisit - Do I taste my words before I speak them." There it was looking right back at me. The pause I took to feel that response from within, made me stop and look at that note on my computer. How did this response taste? It tasted like a big ol' bowl of passive aggressive topped off with righteousness. My HERwithin was getting my attention because this is the exact behaviour I avoid now. I was falling back into old patterns. This person didn't participate in the transitions that I've gone through over the past four years so I was reverting back to my previous behaviour with them. After sitting with my phone in my hand a while longer, I deleted the response. It did feel good to type it out and get it out of my system, but it wasn't the response they deserved. My final response was as simple as "Not offended" along with an inside tip on how to help some stitches heal.

We all know what it's like to react to someone without tasting our words. That programmed response that sounds like our parents doesn't sit far from the surface. I know my sons have heard those trigger reactions before. That's probably why I got so many eye rolls. It's our responsibility to taste our words and be responsible for our experiences. Imagine if that was the way of the world? Remember this the next time you hear a mother yell those canned phrases at her children, or a sports fan who's a little too wound up in the game. It's important to take a breath or a step back and taste our words. If they actually had a flavour or texture to them, what would yours taste like?

FINDING *Her*
NEXT STEPS

1. Those three questions to ask yourself before you speak is the greatest tip I ever received. You'll start off slowly, probably having to refer to your phone as a prompt, but soon the questions will spring up like an internet pop up. Program yourself to ask yourself those questions when you feel the need to be right emerging. You'll know that feeling before you say anything. Learn to recognize it and you'll save yourself a lot of time, arguments and especially energy.

2. What programmed responses can you delete? Those are the things you've heard all your life or picked up from somewhere that influence your behaviours. Remember canned responses are habitual and are reactions, not responses. Responses are created with intention. Next time you're in conversation, make note of the things that come out of your mouth that have no thought attached to them. Even those little fillers that you through into a conversation. One that I am conscious of eliminating is anything that involves the word "should". Maybe it's just a word you use a lot that needs to be deleted. When you say it, write it down. Call yourself out so you can start making the changes you're wanting to make.

3. There's power in The Pause in any conversation. This can be a shock to the people in your life if you're normally a talker. It's also seriously uncomfortable at first. I had one

person ask me if I was having problems putting together a sentence. After the shock and laughter subsided, I explained that I don't have to respond to everything. Pauses in conversations freak people out when it's not a normal thing and you can almost see the internal judgement meter going off. What the other person does within that pause is their responsibility, not yours. The Pause gives you time to ask yourself the three questions or redirect your energy to an appropriate response instead of an instant reaction. This will take time to implement and when you do, take the time to take a nice cleansing breath in and congratulate yourself on using the Power of the Pause.

What bubbled up?

What's your V.I.B.E?

QUESTION #5

How do I participate in conversations?

Have you ever witnessed yourself within a conversation? I mean, stepped back and listened to yourself? In a group of friends, I'm usually the quietest one because I didn't think I had anything important to say. Now I'm aware of what I'm saying, how I say it and the energy I emit while saying it. While I may not say much in a group setting, I tend to leave a positive vibration after I speak.

Do you ever get into a common setting like coffee with a friend or family dinners, and you let your energy fall into a normal rut as if you're engaging in conversations that may have a routine about them? Let's explore coffee with a friend. If you meet at the same place, same time, have the same drink and gossip about the same people, you're on auto pilot. The same ol' same ol' creates the same actions. What would happen if you decided not to gossip about someone over the next coffee? What would you talk about? I took this thought into that coffee with a friend setting and I was surprised by the reaction I got. I'm not one to make people feel uncomfortable and question what they say, but this time I did. By sitting back and giving your energetic power away to someone during a conversation, you are also giving them the power to control the conversation. If you don't question what they say, when it doesn't align with you, that means you agree with them. This particular time, I didn't agree. I was told that I was acting like a victim with my breast cancer because I talked about it so much. I disagreed and explained that I talk about my journey because I'm healing. That called forth an interesting facial expression that I would normally leave alone. This time I asked a question instead of giving away my conversational power. I said, "what's that face for?" and was met with a shocked look. I don't think I've ever questioned what this person would say to me. I wasn't fully participating in the conversation if I allowed these things to happen in the past. The routine of our conversation just hit a major disruption.

Our brain is wired for routine, so you don't have to think so much. It's like getting in your car, starting it, backing out of the driveway and driving down the street. These actions don't take much thought because they make up a routine you do all the time. Conversations shouldn't be routine... unless you have a teenager and you must repeat yourself twenty times. Conversations are exchanges that happen everywhere. From holding open a door and receiving a thank you, ordering a coffee or texts about dinner. What is your level of participation in a conversation?

I created the acronym V.I.B.E. one day while I was witnessing all the ways my energy was being affected during a very one-sided conversation. V.I.B.E. stands for Values, Integrity, Boundaries and Energy. During a conversation, your V.I.B.E. can shift depending on how much power you're giving away. You can unintentionally shift someone else's V.I.B.E. as well, as I did in that previous conversation, when I questioned a response. Throughout this book I talk about all of the components of V.I.B.E. Once you understand how you relate to your values, integrity, boundaries, and energy individually, the power of your V.I.B.E. becomes stronger. Your V.I.B.E. can shift by being triggered, vulnerable or powerless, but you can also shift it back when you understand what's happening to you. When you feel an energetic shift in your body, one of the components of your V.I.B.E. is being affected. Learning about the energy shifts in your body is like finding an instruction manual and you can learn more about that in Question #8.

A friend once told me that while sitting at her desk, she could smell the slight trace of the perfume of a fellow employee she needed to chat with, which meant she was in the building. When she saw her co-worker, she mentioned that she could smell her lovely perfume and knew she was around to chat with. Her co-worker took that comment as criticism about the amount of perfume she was wearing. In this case, my friend was just commenting, in a courteous manner, and the co-worker was triggered. Is it because the co-worker is aware of the strong scent of the perfume? Had she been talked to about that before? Was she self-conscious about drawing attention to herself? Any of those could have triggered the co-worker or it could have been something completely different. When her co-worker reacted to the comment, that's when my friend started questioning her integrity, boundaries and noticed the energy shift in her body. There was also a shift in values, integrity, boundaries and energy for her co-worker. When the trigger is deep, the V.I.B.E. shift is just as deep.

If you feel an energy shift while in conversation, check in with your V.I.B.E. Are you aligned with your values? Are you speaking with integrity? Are you enforcing your personal boundaries? How does your energy feel? Your V.I.B.E will regulate how you participate in conversations. Tune in to it.

FINDING *Her*

NEXT STEPS

1. Take a step back from conversations and listen. You can learn more from listening than from contributing when you're in the midst of Finding HER. What's the energy of the conversation? What's the intention of the conversation? How does the conversation feel? Does this conversation need to end or move somewhere else? You may need to go into drone mode and hover over the conversation for a bit to really get the feel of it.

2. Tune into your V.I.B.E. and the V.I.B.E. of the others in the conversation. When your values, integrity, boundaries or energy are affected, there's something not aligning with you and HER. Those energy shifts are like an internal road flare going off. There's something wrong and your HERwithin is trying to get your attention. Pay attention and make notes. When you start to feel your V.I.B.E. shifts, you'll start changing your interactions, which in turn, will trigger reactions from those in your conversations. Change creates more change so be aware of the domino effect.

3. Take the new awareness's that you've learned about and feed them into your conversations. Take responsibility for your experiences in a conversation. Give more in a conversation. Taste your words before you speak and you'll find your participation in conversations to be more rewarding for you and interesting shifts for those you talk with.

Thoughts & Feelings

Are the people you're

dropping and running for

doing the same for you?

QUESTION #6

What are my expectations of others?

We all have expectations, and you can call it whatever you want. When I think of expectations, I think of control and when the following experience happened to me, I knew right away that I was in a pattern of expectations and control. My husband needed to do some work on his car so I offered to pull mine out of the garage so he could do the work. I gathered my stuff to go grab some groceries and left. In my mind, I would pull away, he would move his car into the garage, and he could work on it there, vacuum it, or do whatever he needed. When I got back, I would park in his spot in the driveway, so I wasn't in the way when he needed to get out of the garage. Perfect plan, right? In my mind, it was wonderful and efficient, and slightly controlling. I returned home to find his car in the same place. He had never moved it. He was supposed to move his car into the garage so I could park in the driveway. That was my expectation. Now I couldn't park on the driveway because I'd be right next to his car and in the way. I couldn't park in the garage because I'd be in the way of his tools and stuff. So now, I had to park on the street. Why didn't he just do what I "expected". His mind-reading sonar must have been turned off that day. A perfect example of a pattern of expectations.

I used to have high expectations of others because I needed to be in control and in turn, I had high expectations of myself. I will admit, it still flares up periodically, but my level of expectation of others has diminished. Why? Because frankly, it's unfair. Unless I have set out exactly what I would like to happen, and it's factual and necessary, there's no need to expect anyone to do anything. My husband doesn't expect me to cook every night, do the laundry or clean the house and I don't expect that of him. We do expect each other to be respectful, courteous and loving unless something actual presents itself to challenge those expectations. When it comes to big family dinners, I have removed any expectations of what others should be doing. If I need help, I ask for it. It's as easy as that. If you expect things to happen, you will undoubtedly end up disappointed.

It's unfair to expect others to act a certain way when something is happening to you. To get angry at someone because they didn't do what you expected them to do is unfair. You don't know what's going on in their world. If you need them for something, ask them. When you are hurting from the loss of a loved one, it's easy to expect others to come to us. For instance, when my mum passed away, I had zero expectations of what my friends should be doing for me. When the word "should" enters any conversation, that's a way of saying that you know better than the other person. "You should have called or come by!" That expectation is the story in your head. An expectation is defined as the act of expecting. When you look at "you should have called or come by" and change the words a little, it means the same thing, but it's all about you this time. "I expected you to call or come by!" The person responsible for this expectation is clearly you, not them. Placing the blame on someone else to do or say something is still your expectation. Changing the statement to start with "I expected …" isn't as easy to say is it?

I experienced a major life changing event in the summer of 2019. I was diagnosed with breast cancer (or Edna as I so lovingly referred to it). Thankfully Edna was found early, didn't spread, and I had her removed within 6 weeks of the first sighting. As I'm writing this, there's still a lot more to go through and I am grateful to be surrounded by love and energy from everyone who knows me. This could have been the perfect opportunity for me to be sitting on a throne of expectations. I have cancer! Everyone needs to come and visit, send me flowers, make meals, drive me places and meet my expectations. Instead, I entered into this life-changing event with zero expectations and I was positively overwhelmed with what happened over an extended period of surgeries and recovery. I was also astonished by the reactions of others. Friends that I've known for years never called, came by or sent a message. Rather than feeling unloved, I sent them love because, in my mind, they were having troubles dealing with this situation I was in. Even family members retreated and didn't know what to say or do. If I had expectations, I would have been wounded by all the silence. Instead, I bathed in the love and energy that was being sent to me. Every day, I'd get a message or a text or a call. Social media is the best place to ask for love and support when going through something big. Reach the masses and let it all flood in. I didn't expect people to respond but, when they did, I usually ended up in tears and my heart was full. I was being showered with so much love. My posts would be more information updates than calls for love and support. I taught myself how to receive love. I pictured each person as I read their response. "Zero expectations" was my motto.

However, there was still bewilderment from the fact that people close to me were M.I.A. I still had an expectation, or maybe it was just hope. I told myself that they were dealing with this news the way they had to. I've done that before. When everyone is flocking to a funeral, I can't. I have my time alone and then I reach out to the family after the flurry has calmed down. That's how I deal with it. The absence of certain people was a lesson for me. I started reflecting on relationships and realized that I was the one who was the giver and even a life event like this wasn't about to change things. I saw a social media post that said: "Are the people you drop and run for doing the same for you?" With zero expectations and a bit of a broken heart, I had a life lesson handed to me. My hopes were based on what I do for others. I hoped that people would treat me the way I would treat them if they were faced with news like mine. Expectations of others is your hot potato to hold. The next time you feel an expectation bubbling up, can you say to someone, "I expected you to..."?

FINDING *Her*
NEXT STEPS

1. Check in with the story you've created in your mind. Chances are, you're the only one that knows the plot. If nobody knows what you're thinking, nobody knows what's supposed to happen. Men aren't the only ones that can't read minds. Make sure you communicate your hope for what could happen. Hopes are expectations without the attachment to the outcome. As soon as an expectation story starts to get out of control, erase it. Those are the stories of victims. You can't be a victim if you communicate your story with love and intentions.

2. If you're going to have expectations, make sure you word your conversations appropriately. You need to take responsibility for your experiences (Remember Question #1?) Since this is your expectation, the conversation you have will start with "I expected you to...". You are taking responsibility now and you won't be pushing the blame on others. When you say "You should have ...", you're pushing the blame on someone else for an expectation you had.

3. Make a list of all the people you have expectations of. These are uncommunicated thoughts that you have an attachment to. Expectations that someone is going to do something, say something, or be something that you're creating in your mind. Write down the person's name and what your expectation is or was. Then, put that list away for a few days. Now that you're aware of the issues

around expectations, you have an awareness that wasn't present before. When you're in a grounded good place, pull that list out again and look at what you wrote. Is it fair for you to think that way about someone? Is it fair for you to impose your expectations on someone else? Can you now tell that person what you're thinking without having an attachment to the outcome? If you can, you've now shifted into hope and out of expectation.

What did you reveal?

A WHYs conversation
can help you get to the root
of a trigger.

QUESTION #7

Why am I triggered?

This is one deep rabbit hole to start going down, but if you're aware that you're being triggered, it's a huge step forward. Sometimes you may react to things like a short-circuiting wire, other times it's a deep hurt that just keeps festering within you as you push down the energetic reaction you're having. Understanding the why around triggers is like opening Pandora's Box. You have to want to understand why it's happening, because one trigger may cause a chain reaction.

A WHYs conversation can help get you to the root of your trigger. The simple act of asking yourself questions brings awareness to the fact that this is your issue, not theirs.

1. Ask yourself a question

2. Answer the question

3. Turn your answer into a 'why' question

4. Repeat until you have answered 5 Why Questions.

Let me share a personal example of my most significant trigger and the reaction that followed;

My trigger: I feel uncomfortable when one of my husband's kids walks in the room!

1. Why do I feel uncomfortable when they walk in the room? His focus shifts to them and I start creating a story in my head that they're interrupting on purpose and you can feel the tension in the air.

2. **Why** do I feel tense? Because this is my time with him, and I don't want to share it with others.

3. **Why** don't I want to share him with others? Someone else took my first husband's attention away from me and I was put on the back burner.

4. **Why** is it hard to share attention? What's going on? I'm an adult, but something is going on around being second.

5. **Why** do I have an issue about being second? The story that I'm telling myself is that being second means that I'm not important. THEN, the big question... WHERE HAVE I FELT LIKE THIS BEFORE? In my first marriage, I always felt like there was something or someone ahead of me. I was right.

With help from an energy healer, I went deeper into my why questions and found the root of where it all started. For me, it started when I was 5 years old, and my younger sister was born. What used to be the focus on me was shifted to a newborn. My ego didn't know what was going on, so it told me "you aren't important" and I held that self-limiting belief for 50 years. I love my sister to pieces, and this never affected us but I'm so glad that I pulled it up and out. This issue was in my belief system. I continually work on it when new situations occur, because now I know I can put that fire out very quickly. Update on children wanting their dad's attention; I don't have any issues with anyone taking my husband's attention away because I know I'm his number one and so are they. The trigger is gone and there's room for everyone in my heart.

As an adult, maturity provides you with the experience and

knowledge that something is ok or not, but when I was faced with this situation and instantly pointed fingers, my conscious self was somewhat confused. That buried self-limiting belief was the truth in my subconscious. If I kept pointing fingers at the one that I thought was the issue, I never would have faced that shadow and released it from my orbit! That trigger was affecting far more than one situation. My subconscious had painted this person with a giant stroke of one color and it didn't matter what else happened.

There's a social model called the Drama Triangle that was conceived by Stephen Karpman. In this model, there is a Victim, a Rescuer and a Persecutor. Think about any conflict you've had and see where you might find yourself based on these descriptions.

The Victim: The Victim's stance is "Poor me!" The Victim feels victimized, oppressed, helpless, hopeless, powerless, ashamed, and seems unable to make decisions, solve problems, take pleasure in life, or achieve insight. The Victim, if not being persecuted, will seek out a Persecutor and also a Rescuer who will save the day but help to perpetuate the Victim's negative feelings.

The Rescuer: The rescuer's line is "Let me help you." A classic enabler, the Rescuer feels guilty if they don't go to the rescue. Yet their rescuing has negative effects: It keeps the Victim dependent and gives the Victim permission to fail. The reward derived from this rescue role is that the focus is taken off of the rescuer. When they focus their energy on someone else, it enables them to ignore their own anxiety and issues. This rescue role is also significant because their actual primary interest is really an avoidance of their own problems disguised as concern for the victim's needs.

The Persecutor: (a.k.a. Villain) The Persecutor insists, "It's all your fault." The Persecutor is controlling, blaming, critical, oppressive, angry, authoritarian, rigid, and superior.

I put myself in the position of Persecutor AND Victim and that always put my husband in the Rescuer position. I remember having a story in my head that I was being victimized by someone's actions. The interesting point is that the other person wasn't doing anything intentionally. They simply walked into the room.

That was a clue that I was being triggered. As soon as I feel like a victim, it's time to find out why. When you are whole, you don't fall into any of those three positions. You sit in the middle of the triangle, and you're not triggered or affected. That's the goal.

Take responsibility for your experiences and take the 10,000-foot level view at something that gives you an energy shift. Where did you feel it? How intense was it? When did my mood change? What was happening? Go within and search for the precise trigger. Ask yourself over and over, "when did I last feel this upset, when did I last feel this upset, when did I last feel this upset?" Allow your memory to bring up any situation that felt the same. You'll be surprised when you remove your armour, and allow HER to help you. You will find out why you're triggered.

FINDING *Her*

NEXT STEPS

1. Finding your trigger point takes a lot of internal recognition and understanding. Using the WHYs conversation whenever you're triggered is the best homework you can do in that moment. If you are unable to ask yourself those why questions, make a note of the situation. If you can note it in your phone or write it down somewhere, you can come back to it later. Trust me, you won't forget that you were triggered. That trigger point came from deep within you. It's there until you face it, erase it and move on.

2. Next time you're in a conversation that could possibly put you in a position of the Victim, Persecutor or Rescuer, become aware of it. Use the tools you've learned so far to remove the level of participation you're having in this situation. Ask yourself the three questions from Question #4. Does this need to be said? Does this need to be said now? Does this need to be said by me? Those questions alone will take you out of one of those three positions and put you in the neutral zone in the middle. Take responsibility for your experiences! If you've said or done something that caused a problem, take a deep breath, ask you protective ego to step aside and rewrite the script for this play on your life stage.

3. Start to track where in your body you feel these triggers. Is there an energetic shift in your body? Do you have a physical symptom that appears? Is the sensation stronger with some people than others? Get curious about how your body reacts

to being triggered. Mental, emotional, energetic, physical and spiritual bodies can all be affected. The more you understand about your bodies, the more you understand about yourself.

What bubbled up?

Emotion is your body putting

your energy in motion.

QUESTION #8

Am I aware of the energy shifts in my body?

While I was writing this book, I had all sorts of flashbacks to the way I used to be. I had no idea what an energy shift was in my body back in 2016. I had emotions and reactions and that was just the way it was. Someone pissed me off, I knew what my reaction would be. Someone hurt me, I knew what my reaction would be. I didn't realize at the time that those emotions are actually energy in motion. Those tears and anger were energetic shifts in my body. You know the saying, "you don't know what you don't know until you know it"? At that time, I didn't know anything about energy. To me, energy was what powered my two sons through hockey, soccer, volleyball and tackle games in the living room. That is energy in motion. Literally. The energy in motion within us is what causes an emotion (E + MOTION = Energy in Motion) and is something that can be felt instantly but, many times, is ignored.

Have you ever watched a movie and wanted to cry but you stopped the tears? Do you remember a time when you were so angry about something and wanted to scream but you stopped it? That's a natural movement of energy that wants out. When you stop emotions from escaping, you're preventing energy from moving. When that energy is connected to a highly emotional event and you choose to suppress it, the body holds onto that energy and encapsulates it because you told it to. The body then finds a new place to set up shop with that energy, because it wasn't allowed to release.

These experiences have intrigued me so much that I'm now incredibly fascinated with the world of metaphysics and the mind, body, and soul connection.

Understanding the connection between the mind and the body is powerful. The first step is recognizing that there's an energetic shift happening within your body. Your ego, or conscious state, will do everything it can to make you think that it's something else that's happening. Through meditation and learning to tune into your body, you can become more self-aware and begin to recognize the energetic shifts instantly, understanding why these shifts happen. You know that 'punch in the gut feeling' when something bad happens or is about to happen? That's an energetic shift. Once you establish a connection to a shift happening, you can then ask why is it happening? Is this related to a trigger? Review the Five Why questions in Question #7 to see if it's a trigger. Is it an emotional reaction to something that makes you sad? Release that energy and allow yourself to cry. The important lesson is becoming aware of energy shifts in your body. Cry if your body wants to release sadness, punch a pillow or growl if you need to release anger. Whatever it is, take responsibility for your own experience and help move the energy through your body.

After the loss of my mum in 2016, I became very emotional every year on the day of her passing. Since it also landed two days after her last birthday, I gave myself permission to mourn. Yet, even though I knew I was going to have a few emotional days, I would preoccupy myself with everything from extended meditation to making soup to writing this book. I was getting very good at avoiding emotion in my head. Then one day, during these rough days in April, my husband came in to ask me if I wanted some lunch and guess what?

I wasn't distracted any longer and the guard had left the gate wide open for the tears to start rolling. I was trying to suppress the energy and emotion my body wanted to release and when I wasn't armoured up and on guard, it found a small opening and escaped. The whole release took about fifteen minutes. When it's allowed to release, it can be a very efficient and cleansing experience.

Probably the most profound shift I ever felt was over a microwave. Yes, a microwave. I've wanted an over the range microwave for years. You know the kind that's mounted on the wall above your stove? I really wanted to have that space on the counter, where the current white microwave sits, as an area for the coffee maker and cookie jar. The day came when we could take advantage of Black Friday deals, and we headed off to pick up the one we'd been looking at.

What I didn't know was this microwave would be a catalyst of sorts. It was about to open a doorway that I needed to walk through. Our drive was sprinkled with some giggles about drivers and melting snow puddles. It was an outing as well as a shopping mission. First, let me back up the SUV and give you some more details.

At the end of October, my husband severely damaged his knee. Movement was limited and the couch became his best friend with his sidekicks Ice Pack and Heating Pad. Poor guy hadn't had a healthy day in almost 6 weeks. It was time for him to get out into the sunshine. So, we went to buy our microwave.

We got front row parking, "Princess Parking" as I call it, and made our way into the store. With the clicking of his crutches on the tiled floor, we wove our way through the Christmas wonderland display (didn't have to go that way but I wanted to) and down to the appliances department. We found the microwave, found a salesperson, got said microwave brought to us and then taken up front until we were ready. We moved through the checkout process flawlessly and then off to the car. I think that's when something happened.

I've done a boatload of changing over the past few years and nobody has seen the unfolding, peeling and transforming the way my husband has. If I could convince him to tattoo a gold medal on his chest, I would. The man is a saint. He was on crutches and couldn't push the cart with microwave balanced across the top. I graciously took the handle of the shopping cart and across the slightly melted snow, I go like the woman in charge. I could feel something bubbling up. Something was shifting and I wasn't sure what it was but, I don't ignore things anymore. If they want up, I let them bubble up and out. We get to the SUV; open the back and I position the cart so I can manhandle that microwave right into the back of the vehicle. Uh oh... it's coming up even higher now. My husband said he'd go put the cart in the cart parking lot and I took it from him and ordered him into the car. I honestly felt like I was possessed. What the hell is going on? As I walked the cart over, I started to feel emotion on the move. Look out!! She's gonna blow! I got back to the car, sat down and burst into tears.

I realized I was acting like the old me. I felt so disconnected from HER at that moment that it scared the hell out of me. I had worked tirelessly finding that piece of me that was missing. It was HER, and I didn't like the conflict I was experiencing. To give you some reference, I'm triggered by women who do everything. The martyrs of the world. I used to be one. I had no problem being one in the past because I didn't trust people. I was a controlling individual that disguised it as organized and efficient (confession time!). I was doing something that generally my husband would do, and I had an emotional reaction. The energy in my body was pushing something up. At the time, I was so confused. Was I reacting to having to move that microwave myself or was I reacting to how I honestly didn't like being a martyr but chose to anyway?

As I sat and cried and hyperventilated a bit (that was weird in itself), I could feel myself calming down. I was facing another shadow head-on. I don't have to be that person any longer. I'm loved, trusted, respected and heard. I'm not sure I have an absolute answer about what happened that day. I don't have to control anything or anyone. As I was moving the microwave, I think my mind was having a flashback and my HERwithin was having an "it's okay, you're okay" moment, and the two of them collided. In the end, the message I was receiving from HER had a lasting impact as opposed to the freak-out moment that my ego created. This was a lesson for me in observing my energy shift and in the power of that quiet voice from within. HER voice is a whisper but is far stronger than the flashing scenes from the past that my ego was throwing at me like pop-ups on my browser.

When you Find HER, you change. You can Feel HER and Hear HER. When you receive messages like I did, honour HER at that moment by talking it through, let your emotions bubble up and out and use the universe's clean up crew of tears to wash away what no longer serves you. When you face the shadows with HER, you have a better chance of clearing them out of your mind and your past. I feel better for that moment and I'm not embarrassed when they happen. That's one shadow that won't be back to bother me ... all because we bought a microwave.

FINDING *Her*

NEXT STEPS

1. Let's get that energy moving!

Step 1 - Find a pillow or basket of clean laundry to muffle the energy you're about to release.

Step 2 - Turn on some music.

Step 3 - Insert your face into muffling device.

Step 4 - Let loose! Scream, cry or punch and let that energy out. It's like opening the flood gates to get that energy out and it will feel amazing!

2. Become aware and curious again. Record energetic shifts that you feel happening. Say something to yourself to acknowledge what's happening and allow it to. When you are aware and acknowledge it, things become real. Also become aware of when these shifts happen and why. What's the trigger? Keeping notes in this book, at the corresponding chapter, allows you to revisit what you did and your lessons you learned. If journaling scares you, look at it as just taking notes.

3. Releasing energy helps you make the changes to your behaviours and emotions that you're craving. Imagine yourself as an over-inflated tire. Releasing the unnecessary air will take the pressure off the structure of the tire. You're over-inflated right now with energy. With a

gradual energy release, in so many areas of your life, you start to feel the energetic shifts more authentically. Once you start releasing, it might be hard to shut that valve off, but don't be afraid to start. You won't cry forever and you'll feel relief, free and happier the more you do it.

Thoughts & Feelings

Thoughts & Feelings

Vulnerability is essential
to allow your inner light
to shine.

QUESTION #9

Am I willing to become vulnerable and face my shadows?

WARNING! If you're a person who loves being in control, you are not going to like this question.

Being vulnerable or showing vulnerability is viewed as being unguarded. It's about dropping your armour and allowing truth to flow through you. Merriam-Webster dictionary defines it as: capable of being physically or emotionally wounded. Capable is the keyword here when you're dealing with your own stuff. You are capable. You aren't going to wound yourself intentionally emotionally when you face your shadows. It may be uncomfortable and the outcome may not be what you expect or desire, but without doing this work you really cannot move forward.

Your next question is probably, "what are my shadows?" You hold both dark and light sides within you. Your light side is the place where you set intentions, watch for signs, meditate, experience laughter, love and joy. Your dark side is where you hold fear, judgement, aggression, shame and greed. To open the door to your shadow side, from whichever side you're on, is scary and takes courage and trust to walk through it. Remember that you are never doing it alone. Your strength comes from within and from HER.

The warning I put at the beginning comes from experience. If I rewind to my first marriage, I was in control of everything. I knew what was happening when it was happening and who was involved. This was a survival mechanism because I knew something was happening beyond my control within that marriage. I experienced both light and dark sides regularly but didn't understand what they were at the time. Then came a time when I needed to step beyond the depths of my dark side and experience more light, love and joy on a daily basis. It felt like I was taking off all my clothes and walking naked around a shopping centre. That's how vulnerable I felt. It was not pleasant, but there's good news. As I journeyed further along my path of personal development, I found myself getting stronger and stronger and my shadows that were bubbling up were easily handled.

Then something happened. It was like I crossed over a threshold and the Universe said, "ok, let's start bringing up the big guns. She can handle them now." The first colossal shadow was the limiting belief I had that I wasn't important. That belief alone took hours of meditation, two energy workers plus more journaling and blogging than I've ever done. I admit that I'm not 100% through this particular one. It's had a hold on me for fifty years so I'm not expecting it to move along swiftly. I'm finding that a lot of the limiting beliefs I hold within myself have a root of "I'm not important". I'm more aware than ever and when I feel triggered, I can have a quick team meeting with HER and I'm good in record time. There are many layers to this one. Some are easier to step over and others require a running start to get over.

When I made the leap forward to attend my first retreat, I went based on my intuition. It was the most spontaneous thing I had ever done alone. I heard about this retreat on a podcast and while on the bus one day, I contacted the coach by email. I made the decision to attend this retreat ten days before I had to leave. Shortly after, I was travelling to California alone and attending body movement classes alone and staying in a little bungalow by the ocean, alone. I know now that my HERwithin was jumping for joy because we were about to be reunited. At the time, I was alone.

It was day one of the retreat, and I felt so lost. I truly didn't know who I was any longer. That's when I realized that I had lost contact with my body and my spirit. I knew I was guarded and fully armoured because that's how I protected myself from things beyond my control. When we sat quietly and looked within to comfort ourselves, I was always in tears. There was so much emotion flowing through me and it was the first time in years that I allowed myself to be vulnerable. I wanted to apologize to myself for being so distant. I knew there was a spirit within me that was a higher version of myself. I finally felt like I wasn't alone. I had experienced fifty years of life, on guard and controlling. That connection I found within had a very weak signal and it was going to take more than a weekend retreat to reconnect.

Genuine connection takes time, patience, surrender, trust, boundaries, stillness and vulnerability. Imagine your HERwithin constantly saying "Can you hear me now"? That's what's happening between you and HER when your signal is weak. If you're wearing armour at the same time, that signal can't penetrate those barriers. Vulnerability is essential so your inner light can shine beyond your armour.

Ask yourself if you're willing to become vulnerable and face your shadows. It's a one-woman job, and you're the right person to do it.

FINDING *Her*
NEXT STEPS

1. Baby steps are the best advice I can give you. If you compare becoming vulnerable to getting undressed, you have to do it one step at a time. Take a small step equal to taking off your socks. Take a step to show your vulnerability with the closest person you know. Practice that until you can feel it naturally happening. You'll know when you've taken too big of a step. Your HERwithin will give you nudge in some way. She will also let you know if you aren't being vulnerable enough.

2. Ask Ego to step aside. I've talked about Ego and how it wants to protect you. It will still be doing it here and it'll be on red alert. You're making some big changes. Talk to Ego nicely. Say thank you and ask it to please step aside. You'll start to understand how much Ego stands in your way. If you look at Ego as an entity of its own, and not your personal ego, the division helps to move yourself forward.

3. Be vulnerable with yourself. Ask yourself these questions in the book and allow the truth to surface. Your true answers will come from your soul, not your mind. The answers that are true aren't always the easiest to feel and hear but they are the right ones. By creating a routine, safe space and grounded experience, you can allow your soul to speak to you. The answers you're looking for are within it. Let HER speak to you. Find HER. Trust HER. Love HER.

What did you reveal?

A response can be as small

as a drop of water.

It doesn't have to be an

entire bucket.

QUESTION #10

Do I have boundaries?

I thought boundaries were what kept people out. Like putting up your hand and saying STOP when they get too close to violating something meaningful to you. I first learned about boundaries in that retreat in California. I was faced with the reality that I let people walk all over me, I didn't respect myself enough to stop myself from doing stupid things and, any boundaries I did have wouldn't have held up in a strong wind.

Boundaries are the guidelines that you create so that others understand how to behave around you. Well, that's only one side of it. They are also guidelines that you create so that you understand how you need to behave around others. Boundaries aren't just for the outside visitors to abide by. They're the fortress walls around your being. They're also the limits on how far you will allow yourself to go. They're that giant rubber band that pulls you back when you hit your capacity limit.

When boundaries are created hastily, you'll expose gaps and cracks for your energy to leak through. Have you ever tried to say 'no' to someone but felt your integrity crumbling around you? When your boundaries aren't built on solid ground, with intention, or built for one person in a specific situation, you won't experience the real benefit of a boundary.

Creating boundaries that apply to one person can be a recipe for disaster. When this person does this, I create this boundary.

When that person does that, I create that boundary. Imagine how many boundaries you'd have to create to keep on top of every person you encounter. Boundaries are situational. When this situation occurs, regardless of who it is, this is my boundary.

I came face to face with this realization while learning about my own boundaries. I allowed people to say or do what they wanted, then I would bitch about it to the first person who would listen. I was looking for allies to make myself feel better, but I wasn't looking after myself. Boundaries are the most powerful form of self-care. When you have boundaries in place, you are showing yourself that you are worthy of love, and that love comes from within. Gathering allies to make myself feel better only made me a victim. If I had boundaries in place, I could have stopped that behaviour and protected myself from any kind of harm. The first, and most significant boundary I established, knowingly, is when someone raised their voice at me while I was trying to have a conversation. I would tell them, "I do not allow others to raise their voices at me and this conversation will end now". We could continue talking when they were able to have a calm conversation. It only took ten years of enduring these kinds of conversations for me to step up and say NO MORE! I use this one when I feel threatened or verbally dumped upon.

When I'm being accused of something where the other person is clearly trying to shift the blame, I present another boundary that simply states, "I feel that I'm being blamed for something and that's unfair." I leave the conversation and invite the person to continue once they take responsibility for their experience in the situation. My personal boundaries that I engage for myself are there to stop me from over-giving and feeling resentful. I'm a giver in a big way and once

I realize that my time, money and efforts are being spread too thin, and had become an expectation from others, I start engaging my boundaries. Responses to requests for my time if I'm unavailable, are now limited to "thank you but I'm not available". I used to give an essay response as to why I couldn't do something by laying out my details, feelings and actions to justify why I couldn't be of help. Justifying your energy. A response can be a drop of water, not a bucket full.

When I started looking at boundaries to preserve, maintain or reclaim my energy, it all started to make sense. Remember the energy shifts we talked about in Question #8? Boundaries create containers for our energy. When your boundaries are weak, your energy is affected. Timing is the challenge to establishing boundaries for the first time. From personal experience, I've learned not to create them on the spot when emotions are high. They are doomed to fail. Look at the areas of your life that are closest to you and see if you need some boundaries for your energy. Are you a messy boundary creator that does it just for survival, or are you a rigid boundary creator that has armoured up for battle? The time to create boundaries is when things are good. A casual conversation starter like, "I'm doing some work on myself and I've had some things come up. I'm finding ways I want to show up better. Would you like to hear about it?" This starts the dialogue regarding your boundaries in a less volatile environment.

What boundary do you know you need to establish, in order to protect your energy?

FINDING *Her*
NEXT STEPS

1. Make a list of all the situations that trigger you. Take your time and sift through them all. Now, beside each situation, list the name of the person or people involved. Finally, and this is where the vulnerability comes in, write "because I allowed myself to...". Without pointing fingers at anyone else (Questions #1), what did you allow to happen? Do you see a pattern? The same situations will keep reappearing until you make a change. Most of the time, that involves boundaries for all involved.

2. Practice writing out boundaries that apply to situations. Regardless of who's involved, those boundaries are going to be regular homework for you. I admit, I falter at times with my boundaries because I just don't have the energy to enforce them. That's like telling myself that I'm not important enough. You'll learn to recognize situations that require boundary reinforcement. Over time, you won't have to act on those as often because the people involved are learning that you've changed and you have boundaries for yourself and situations.

3. Stop yourself from gathering allies after a boundary has been crossed. As soon as you find yourself in the victim position, STOP, ask yourself what boundary was crossed and what did YOU need to do differently. No finger pointing. These are your boundaries that have been crossed or haven't been established yet.

What bubbled up?

Fulfillment is about fuelling yourself from within.

QUESTION #11

Why do I feel lost and unfulfilled?

Is it time to look in the mirror and ask yourself if you're faking your way through things? Are you going through the motions and just existing or are you living a life of fulfillment and meaning? If you take the time to ask yourself these powerful questions, be prepared for an energetic shift and whatever bubbles up, let it out! Don't suppress whatever you're faced with. Take the time to settle in somewhere, grab a mirror and ask your HERwithin if you're feeling lost. Then ask HER if you're feeling fulfilled. You may be faced with other questions when you start connecting with HER. You may disrupt some shadows tucked away in your subconscious. Boxes will open, messages, questions and emotions will start coming to the surface. It's like knocking over a giant rock and all the creatures living under it come scurrying out in every direction. Or, you may be so disconnected that you get nothing. If you don't get any response from within and you know you're not on the right track, let it go and try again. Before you go to bed that night, ask yourself if you're living a fulfilling life and let your subconscious chew on that overnight. You may be surprised by what surfaces. If you're a dreamer, keep your journal ready because when you give your subconscious a job, it will fill you with answers.

If you've been at a place in your life where you know something isn't right, but you can't put your finger on it, you may be lost. If you have more questions than answers, you may be living an unfulfilled life. Here's the problem that you face. You continue down your road of life with the same people, jobs, habits and hobbies but when you aren't fully expressing who you are and wandering away from 'home', you feel like you're lost. Home is your HERwithin. Unfulfilling careers are a good sign that you're lacking something that your HERwithin is craving. When you're disconnected from your HERwithin, you deny yourself the things you crave. Imagine what your life would be like if you didn't starve yourself of those things. Take some time to figure out what those things are and why you don't have them.

In the rinse and repeat lifestyle I was living, I changed jobs every two years because I wasn't fulfilled. Some stress leave and a layoff saw me at home for a while where you'd think I would have time to relax and regroup. That wasn't the case. I had a must-do attitude and I wasn't doing! I tried to fill in those career gaps by creating my own companies. I had Beyond the Basics (desktop publishing), Efficient Solutions (Organizing Service) and Emerald Marketing. I had to fill a void within myself. I never made much money at any of them, but I was busy doing something. With the knowledge I have now about mind, body and soul connection, I realize my body and the Universe were trying to tell me something when I was removed from the corporate grind. At the time, all I knew was that I didn't have a purpose. I didn't have a reason to get up, get dressed and go to work. I had gathered a lot of valuable skills and information and I now know my careers weren't aligned with my values and beliefs. That became very apparent in my last job when my body started to send me very distinct signals of distress.

My mum's passing in 2016, as I shared before, was THE crossroads for me in many aspects. I knew I needed to make a life change, or I'd regret moving forward in my own journey. I left the job I had at the time and started working on my personal development. I needed to find the answers to all these questions bubbling up from within. At the time, I didn't know the answers weren't on the internet or in one of the many self-help books I bought or lingering within a podcast. I learned that everything I needed to know was already within me. My answers had always been there. I worked with a couple of coaches who helped guide me to my answers and when I found the source, it was like finding a cave of wonders. Everything I ever wanted was right at my fingertips.

The next step was to figure out what I needed to create the fulfilling life I wanted. My fulfillment wasn't coming from my husband, children, family or friends. When lack of fulfillment is felt to the core, there's a void that needs filling. Remember Question #2 about giving and receiving? I was giving in the hopes that it would make me feel better and fill that void within me. Instead, I learned about all the ways that I wasn't looking after myself. My lack of fulfillment was because I wasn't fueling myself with love. This is a different love than the one you get from others. This is a divine love that's like a bright light burning within yourself. As a mum, I knew my bright light was down to a burnt ember. It was going to take a lot of oxygen to get that ember into a full flame again. I learned about boundaries and reclaiming my own energy. I learned about trust and preserving my energy. I learned about putting down unnecessary baggage and maintaining my energy. Fulfillment is all about fuelling yourself from within. Nobody has the answers to why you're feeling unfulfilled and lost, but you.

During an energy healing session to help me release some buried treasures of self-limiting beliefs, my healer asked me an interesting question. She asked me if I'm connected to love within myself. I took that as if she was asking me if I was connected to my HERwithin. Without hesitation, I answered yes, but as it came out, there was an inflection at the end. My yes was more of a question. Ego had one answer, but my HERwithin had another answer. I must be connected within. I am HERwithin. How can I not be connected to love within?

After more discussion, I admitted that I'm technically connected. I explained that the connection I feel is like taking two computer wires and attaching them. There's an electrical connection I have that brings HER more to the forefront. I have more awareness and allow HER to connect with me. But, was I connected to love within? She explained that we come from Source or Divine Love. I'm still deciphering all that, but I think I understand it. When you're at the beginning of your life journey, you're fully connected to Source or Divine Love. You are Love without conditions. As soon as you become the seed that creates you, that's when you start picking up energy from others. When you pick up that energy, your pure love from Source starts to cloud. In utero, you pick up your mother's energy, her self-limiting beliefs and fears. The clouding is already beginning. Then as you grow and learn, you take on other's rules and beliefs until you're old enough to determine those for yourself. Even at that point, you can still be influenced. So that pure love you started with gets cloudier and cloudier, and it's no wonder you feel lost and unfulfilled. You have drifted so far from home and your source of love, that there becomes a void where that pure love used to be. That's why finding your stillness within is so important. I found this even more critical as I reached midlife. That's the time when I started asking myself those deeper questions about fulfillment and purpose.

By midlife, I knew I was lost and feeling unfulfilled, but I didn't know what to do to fix it. I knew that changing careers wasn't the answer. I knew I couldn't find it from anywhere else and I knew the answers were within me. Great! Now what? Finding my connection to my love within sounded like the right path to take to get to my answers. Unfortunately, love wasn't a deep well for me so I was a bit concerned about what I'd find down there. The surprise discovery came during my healing time after breast cancer. It wasn't a love for the people who cared for me that started to fulfill me. It was a universal love. Love as an energy was flowing from within me. The more I tapped into it, the stronger it got. Imagine taking a lid off a box of butterflies. At first one or two fly out and then word gets out that the lid is off and the flurry of fluttering butterflies begins. That's the only way I describe the feeling that kept building within me. That fulfillment brought me to a place where I no longer felt lost. Wherever I was, I was filled with love. I could sit in a chair and overflow with love. I could be washing my hands and I felt love. It wasn't directed at anything; it was just love. I know that I had to live through love in order to complete my journey with HER and embody the essence of my journey. My tag line for HERwithin is Find HER, Trust HER, Love HER. You are reading Find HER. I've started writing Trust HER but I couldn't wrap my head around Love HER. Now I can. I am no longer lost and unfulfilled in the sense of my being. Sure, I have days when I wonder if I'm missing something in my life, but that is easily replaced with the love I have within.

The next time you're wondering if this is all there is or if there's more somewhere else, look in the mirror and ask yourself if you're feeling lost or unfulfilled and then wait for the answers from within.

FINDING *Her*

NEXT STEPS

1. Take the time to look deep into your own eyes, past the ego, masks and fear and ask yourself if you are feeling unfulfilled or lost. When you talk to your soul, it will answer with emotion that you've been avoiding. Ask, release the emotion and keep asking until you feel relief.

2. What are you avoiding? Are you keeping busy so you don't hear the messages from within? If you consider yourself high energy, a people pleaser, an extrovert or really sociable, you may be avoiding those emotions within. Being busy isn't always fulfilling. Having your day mapped out doesn't mean you're not lost. Slow down, breathe and listen. Don't be afraid to hear what your HERwithin has to say.

3. What's your love life with yourself? Internal love is the most fulfilling aspect of being a human. You're like a self watering plant when you know how to do it. For all that love that you send out to the world and the people around you, save some for yourself and feed your soul with the one thing that created it. LOVE! Self love is self fulfillment.

Thoughts & Feelings

Trust that what you get
from HER is what you need.

QUESTION #12

Do I trust or control?

Prior to my awakening, my road map for life was basically a highway named Control with a few roadside turnoffs called Trust. As far as I was concerned, everything was just fine until I noticed that my main highway was actually a pitted gravel road and not as smooth a ride as it was intended to be. What does yours look like?

I came to the realization that my ability to be efficient and organized was just a disguise for being controlling. While I am still a very highly efficient and organized person, I've learned to release any attachment to the outcome of things. We host family dinners here with twelve people and I trust that whoever was looking after setting the table, serving drinks or bringing food, was capable. I don't need to be in control of everything that happened. I trust them. If someone forgets to bring the veggies or wine, it's not the end of the world. I can say that now, but when I was in the depths of my controlling martyrdom, nobody could tell me it would be ok if something was missing or the table wasn't perfect.

The table below depicts a great comparison I made up to remind myself if I was starting to fall back into my controlling ways. The table shows similar variables for trust and control and at what level they need to be at to reflect trusting or controlling.

CONTROLLING	**VARIABLE**	TRUSTING
HIGH	ATTACHMENT	LOW
LOW	FLUIDITY & FLEXIBILITY	HIGH
HIGH	NEED TO BE RIGHT	LOW

Think of the last time you had to collaborate with others to get something done. At work, at home or even in an emergency. Which column did you fall into? I distinctly remember how I used to insist that things had to be put in an exact place in a drawer. Not just in the drawer, which now I see as a win, but in an exact place inside the drawer. One day, I dumped out a drawer onto the counter and threw everything back into the drawer in total disarray. I remember thinking to myself, if they won't do it my way, then have fun finding anything. I still laugh at the thought of doing that. Did I have an attachment to the outcome of the drawer every single day? YES! Was I flexible about the drawer? NO! Did I have an intense need to be right regarding the placement of the utensils? YOU BET! What it took was to clean out the drawer, explain where things went, and now that drawer is a functioning part of a happy household. Can you see how expectations were removed when communication opened up?

Where in your orbit do you have a high attachment to the outcome? Is it worthy of an energetic investment or as my husband used to say, is this a hill you want to die on? When you run questions like that through your own filters, you can get confused with the answers. Ego will make sure it's the first one to answer. If it's not done this way, you're going to die! It must be done this way. There's no other way. Then give yourself some time to listen for the true answers from within. Chances are you've been programmed along the way that you can't trust it'll be done right. What happens if the potato masher is put in with the small utensils? Will the drawer explode? Reflect on your expectations. Do you expect others to know and understand without having a conversation? Do you know and understand why it must be this way? Raising your fluidity and lowering your need to be right creates harmony and alignment within yourself.

When others know that you don't trust them, conflict and tension will surface, resulting in resentment and bitterness. Is that the result you want? If you google the word Trust, you find these definitions;

- "belief that someone or something is reliable, good, honest, effective, etc."

- "assured reliance on the character, ability, strength or truth of someone or something."

- "one in which confidence is placed."

Do you trust yourself? Do you trust others? Do you trust HER?

To trust, you must release control of the outcome. Letting go of control can be quite a task for some of us. I used to push the boundaries of being organized and in control, with being controlling. I found the difference between these by learning that being organized is factual. Soccer practice is at this time, these files go in the blue filing cabinet, bedtime is at 8:30pm. There are facts that have confirmed results. Well, maybe not bedtime. Being controlling is a "what's best for me" mindset, when you think you know better. "You should wear the red dress, you shouldn't be sitting in that chair, you should tell her that it's none of her business." Tune into your conversations and before you say the word should, ask yourself if you're trying to control the other person or situation. Listen to HER and you won't hear her "shoulding" all over. I had a gathering in my backyard with 6 other women. I purposefully sat back and listened for the word should when one of the women asked for advice about a family matter. The shoulds were flying around like the apple blossoms in the wind. Once I noticed how much should advice was flying around, I purposefully worded my advice with "I" statements. Saying should to someone is telling them that you know better. Do you? Would you follow your own advice?

To trust completely, you must let go of control. These two characteristics are opposites. There is no way you can trust someone or something and still have control of the outcome. Less Control, More Magic (mantra from The Wild Soul Movement) is a wonderful thing. The world is not going to collapse around you if you allow your co-worker to take over a task that you have no time to complete. Your family is not going to starve if you let your daughter help you prepare dinner. I was asked once if I could release control over how the table was set. If the forks were crooked, could I still eat? If the dinner was put into the "wrong" bowl, would it still taste as good? I'm laughing as I'm typing that.

Trusting opens up your ability to receive. Do you have that friend that would give you the shirt off her back but when you try to offer her something, you hear "no that's ok. I'm good". Or is that you? When someone offers to bring you something when you're sick, do you graciously accept or not? How do you feel when you give? Does it fill your heart to help? Maybe it fills the heart of others to help you. Sometimes you forget how the other person feels when they want to give. Be receptive! Trust yourself. Trust others. Let go of the "I got this" martyrdom. Value yourself. Learn to receive graciously. If you're going to be receptive... BE RECEPTIVE! That includes being receptive to criticism. When you do, the roads become two-way with free-flowing traffic. Notice the difference in yourself and then notice the difference in others around you. Notice the difference and most of all, acknowledge it.

Who is in your circles of trust?

When you share, you share it with different people at different levels of intensity. There's no cut and dried organizational chart that outlines your circle of trust. It can be depicted in so many ways. If you look up "circles of trust" online, you'll see they can have any number of circles. The idea is that your people, community and everyone else are organized in such a way that when you have something to share, you already know who will receive what level of detail and emotion.

I have one that I use that came in very handy while dealing with breast cancer. I wanted people to know, but all of them didn't need to know every detail. Even though I had my people in specific circles, there were still some floaters that moved around. I'll explain that in a bit.

I'm a speaker who shares my wisdom wherever I can. Be it through social media or at a microphone, I want people to learn from my journey. I've shared my journey with many people, but the level of intensity (how diluted the information is) differs. It's how you determine your circles of trust that determine what information goes to whom. If you look up Circles of Trust on the internet, you'll find varying diagrams that tell you what you should do. The truth is, it's up to you. Nobody can know for you, and so, you decide how many circles and who to put in them.

The guidelines I use for my own life is as follows (in other words what my circles look like):

The first circle of trust can touch my heart

The second circle of trust can touch my hand

The third circle of trust can touch my home

To explain a bit further, if someone was to make an impact on your life, how deep would the impact be? If it's in my closest entrusted circle, the impact would be felt within. A very personal connection has been created so they would be in my 1st Circle of Trust. Information shared is not diluted.

For those in your second circle, the impact, or how they connect with you takes place at "an arm's length" as the reference to the hand indicates. By keeping these people at arm's length, you are changing the intensity of the information they receive. You have the ability to select what they receive and with whatever intensity you choose.

Your third circle of trust are those beyond your personal connections. These are the people outside of your daily life that receive very diluted information to keep them informed. There can be family in the third circle depending on your relationship with them.

By classifying your circles based on the people in them, it can be confusing when one illustration shows family in the first circle, but you know that there are other people that you trust more than some family. Once you make the decision of who goes into what circles, you have the ability to move them around. Life brings us so many challenges and if you don't take control over who you trust, your heart will be broken and relationships will crumble. Don't put yourself in a position of regret because "that's the way it's supposed to be". You make the rules and decide who knows what. Think of this like a video game where you can pick up a cartoon image of someone and move them to another circle. It's a great visual to use when things change. You have the controls so you make the decisions.

Giving, Receiving & Trust

If you aren't receiving with an open heart, you aren't giving with an open heart. Do you find that you give with conditions attached? Do you loan things to people with conditions on returning or do you trust them to return it? Are you suspicious of people who give you something out of the blue? Take it one step at a time. Learn to receive openly or give openly if this is scary to you.

My aha moment that I was now giving without condition was when my son asked if I had an old iPad or iPod he could borrow. His friend's grandfather was in the hospital with stage 4 throat cancer. Being musicians, they wanted to share some of their music with him before he passed on. I couldn't have thought of a better time to activate my unconditional giving, without control. I handed my version 2 iPad to my son and told him that I want to share this and make the last days of a man's life as pleasant and happy as possible. Grandpa was thrilled and was transported to palliative care... with an iPad to listen to some beautiful music. I never did get it back but not long after, my husband bought me a new one. I gave without condition and my heart opened up even more.

Are you really listening?

You can listen to your body and hear the cracks and moans but are you really listening to your body? Those gut feelings and aha moments, they're your intuition talking to you. When you hear HER communicating with you, stop, become peaceful with yourself and listen to HER communicate with you. You can connect and receive the information with an open heart.

Do you trust HER to guide you in the right direction? Have you ever driven down the same road you always do and know your turn is coming up, but "something" is telling you to turn earlier than usual? It's when you don't listen that you find out why you were being guided in another direction. Something like this happened to me. I was getting into my car and I heard "Macleod to Southland". That's not the regular route I take, and I shrugged it off. I took my normal route and giggled when I was stuck in traffic for twenty minutes due to construction. If I listened to HER, I would have been early for my appointment. What's the saying? "Walk the walk? Lesson received!

Like many women, you might spend a lot of time in your head. Our brain is very chatty and wants to have its say in what you do. Especially if you are being guided by a gut feeling. When your body is screaming a collective YES to an idea or situation, it's your brain that jumps in with the Negative Nancy talk. "Is this the right time to do this? Are you sure you can handle this? What happens if it doesn't work out?" You've all heard this before. Women's intuition is highly talked about for a reason. It's real. Here's an example of how your body knows before your mind does.

Imagine you're out walking your dog. Your dog runs out onto the road while a car is coming. Without even thinking, you scream, your heart is racing, and you run for your dog. Your mind didn't have time to jump in and start asking questions. You reacted to your intuition. Something terrible is about to happen. MOVE IT! It's not until after you've stopped that your mind starts with the questions. "How fast was that car going? How did Murphy get off the leash? Why wasn't I paying attention?" Slowing or stopping the chatter in our head is key to moving into an intuitive state of trusting, receiving and giving. Your intuition comes from within. It doesn't come from your mind.

If you don't trust your intuition, the information that is being sent to you is useless. Trust that what you get from HER is what you NEED. The next time you're faced with a situation where you can either trust or control, what will you do?

FINDING *Her*

NEXT STEPS

1. Take the time to visit your circles of trust. How many circles do you have? What are the names of your circles? Who are in those circles? Once you've determined all of that, set it aside for a week or so. Go back later and revisit what you wrote. If something isn't sitting right, you'll see or feel it right away. You took the time to create the document that represented your levels of trust. Was it created from your ego or from your heart? Was it created from personal values or from the way it's always been? You're the one who decides. Let your answers come from within.

2. Moving from controlling to trusting is not a smooth ride. Trust me on this one! I developed coping mechanisms that helped me divert my controlling responses. Find something that will stop you from reacting. Maybe it's as easy as getting a glass of water. Find a mantra that will draw your attention to something calmer. I use "what does it matter" and say it over and over until the feeling has passed. I heard of someone who spins her tongue around in her mouth ten times until the feeling passes. Don't forget to count!

3. Trust the messages you receive from within. You many not understand or respond to them at first. Remember that you're basically ignoring yourself when you do that. Feeling a gut feeling, hearing a few words or seeing a vision is already happening within you. Trust that it's truly

meant for you to follow. We all have the ability to tap into our intuition, HER, so why are you avoiding it. Trust HER!

What did you reveal?

What did you reveal?

Learn to let go of what was, face what is and ready yourself for what will be.

QUESTION #13

Have I gone through a transition that's still lingering?

You spend your life transitioning. Every time you move through something that has a deep emotional root; you're transitioning. Job changes, disease, birth, death, marriage, divorce, retirement, moving, all of these have an emotional component to them. Many women, including myself, are the masters of pushing down the emotions we don't want to deal with at the time. This will affect the speed of your transition. Think of it as a revolving door. Sometimes they move so fast they clip your heels. Others move so slow it's almost painful and others move at the perfect pace to your stride.

An Ending

The first phase you go through with a transition is An Ending. Something must end before something new can begin, right? William Bridge, author of "Transitions, Making Sense of Life's Transitions", describes five aspects of the natural ending experience; Disengagement, Dismantling, Disidentification, Disenchantment, Disorientation. You experience all of these as you move through the first phase of a transition. It's important to understand each of these and how they assist us in moving forward.

A successful transition requires you to unpack along the way. Imagine this... You move through a transition. You unpack almost everything. Maybe not that thing between you and your mum. Oh, and let's not unpack that resentment issue or the NTBR (need to be right). All those issues are put back in a box and put away in the closet. Now you're moving through another transition. You start unpacking. Hmmm… not going to unpack that control issue over my stuff and probably not going to need to deal with the anxiety. Let's just leave those in this box over here. You stick that away with that other box of issues you didn't want to unpack. Next transition … time to unpack! STOP RIGHT THERE!

When you transition and don't unpack from the last journey, you are bringing unnecessary baggage into a fresh situation. As you move through life, each transition creates more issues that you "pack away". Those issues may seem nicely tucked away, but it will take only one similar situation to create a reaction because they were never dealt with. Do you have any of those lingering pieces from a transition? How many boxes do you have tucked away with unresolved issues in them? Think of the energy it takes for your body to keep repressing these issues. Isn't it time to start unpacking?

The Bridge

The second phase of a transition is The Bridge. This is where all the magic happens, and it's the part that most people avoid because it can feel uncomfortable and probably a little too woo woo for some. Imagine doing NOTHING! Literally, NOTHING! Women may only allow themselves a few minutes at a time, which is a start. This is the time to create space and distance from your old ways. You don't need to replace the old ways with new ways yet. This is an emptiness that is necessary to ensure that the release of the past has happened. Trying to fit your old ways into a new beginning is a recipe for disaster. You need to change and release. Remember to always check in on your emotions. Be aware of what your emotions are wanting to express. Keep that energy in motion, and you'll find this process to be less of an uphill struggle. African tribes create a rite of passage for young men as they journey into adulthood. They remove them from the village and send them out, alone, into the jungle, to release the child and return a man. Allow yourself this rite of passage to release what was, face what is and ready yourself for what will be.

This was the most beautiful part of my transition. I allowed myself the time to reconnect within and undo so many things that were hardwired in me. This wasn't easy because I came from being a Coordinator and always being the hub of everything. It's the perfect position for someone that likes to be in control of things. It was time to let all that go. Sitting on my deck, reading, listening to music, going for walks, learning about crystals and finding new things to eat and drink, to heal my body, was a far cry from maintaining websites, planning events and keeping entire marketing departments organized. It was time for me to learn to breathe, receive and relax.

The New Beginning

The final phase is the New Beginning. When you're ready to step into your New Beginning, one of the first things you'll be faced with is your inner critic, or as International best-selling author, speaker and coach, Martha Beck, calls it, your inner lizard. When I know my inner lizard has entered the game, I kindly ask it to step aside because I've got this. Your inner lizard, inner critic or 'the itty-bitty shitty committee' I've even heard it called, doesn't like change. It wants things to stay the same. That's why it's important to kindly ask it to step aside. It's truly looking out for you based on what your past behaviour has been, but now you need to take action on your new beginning.

How do you take action and make this New Beginning actually

happen? Envision what you want your world to be like. This is your dream to create and for you to step into. What do you see and feel? You will be faced with resistance because this is new. Resist the resistance. When resistance appears, ask yourself these questions:

Is there something I don't want to look at?

Is there something I don't want to be with?

Is there something I don't want to feel?

Is there something I don't want to experience RIGHT NOW?

Stay strong and stop yourself from wanting to turn around and run back to what was. Find your answer within these questions to remove the fear that's surfacing. When you can give one of the something questions an answer, it will leave your orbit, and all will be well with that specific moment. Focus on your goal and the process of reaching your goal. You can do it. You've probably done it before but didn't think so deeply about it.

How many times have I wanted to pack things up and just go back to being someone else's coordinator? I've honestly lost track. It's uncomfortable to take that step into something new, but I wasn't going to go back to another career that would probably only last two years. I had far more to offer the world, and I had to stay true to my course. So, what was holding me back? What part of this transition was lingering and didn't get my full attention? There's no rule that says I can't have a do-over or a second chance to make changes. I went back into An Ending and The Bridge to ensure that I had indeed followed through with the steps. Going through a transition is hard work. Not just on mental and emotional levels but also on a spiritual level. That spiritual connection made during

The Bridge, is teaching you how to strip down and face your fears, worries, self-limiting beliefs and yourself. You can't skim through this part because that's where the magic happens.

What transition have you just gone through? What are you still carrying around from an unprocessed transition? Unpack the stuff you think you need to carry around and look at it. Is it yours? Chances are you've got a lot of someone else's baggage weighing you down. Your goal is to move through your life's journey with just a carry on of joy, love, peace and fulfillment.

FINDING *Her*
NEXT STEPS

1. Look in your purse, your closet, the storage room and your soul. What are you keeping or carrying around that is no longer yours or necessary? Those are the things that tie us to our past. Letting go is hard, I agree, but you need to take the step and look. Avoiding the step of letting go is the foundational step of a transition. You'll never truly move forward if you're carrying other people's stuff around.

2. Take time to physically walk across a bridge and stop half way. Look back at what was, look at what is and look forward to what will be. The time on the bridge is important. This is the point where you've walked far enough away from the past that you can breathe. This is the transitional place that takes you from point A to point B. It's not an easy walk sometimes, but it's a necessary walk. Relate it to spring time. You've left the cold winter behind but it's not time for the heat of the summer (in the northern hemisphere of course). Springtime on the bridge is refreshing, a time of new growth and the spring showers that wash away the past. Use this time wisely and if you skipped over it during a past transition, go back and stand on the bridge.

3. Your new beginning may not feel so refreshing and new if there's still lingering remnants from the past. Remind yourself to let go of the old ways. Don't take the old ways

and try and place them in a new situation. Coming from personal experience, that is a recipe for disaster. Release the habitual dinosaur and let her run back to the past where she belongs. That's not you any longer. Use the tools you've gathered throughout this book to Hear HER, Trust HER and Follow HER.

What bubbled up?

What bubbled up?

Move through life with just a carry-on of your own stuff.

QUESTION #14

How much unnecessary stuff am I carrying around because I won't put it down?

Remember all the boxes and baggage from Question #13? What haven't you unpacked along your journey? We all carry baggage. Much of it is unnecessary stuff that you're carrying because it defines you and if you put it down and walk away, who are you? Right? That thing between you and your mum has been hanging around for way too long. When we take responsibility for our experiences, there is no room for baggage. You can clear up whatever you're involved with so that there are no unanswered questions or doubt. What another person does with their stuff from the same situation is not your problem. You are your own problem and it's time to put some issues to rest and walk away.

Letting go of that baggage requires forgiveness, release and sometimes an apology. Your unpacked boxes hold negative energy that takes up precious space within you. Have you ever been triggered by something someone said and then asked yourself where did that come from? It's trapped negative energy that's looking for a way out. It's the stuff you don't want to think about. When you shove it down, you trick yourself into forgetting about it. But all it takes is one mention of something and 'kablam' you've been triggered!

I remember one situation where this happened to me. The span from when it used to occur, and when it happened again was about 10 years. I was in California with my husband and we were on a road navigating our way back onto the main freeway to head north up the coast. I was trying to navigate using the map on my phone and had myself upside down and backwards. As we sat at a light, and I wasn't navigating fast enough, my husband got a bit, I mean a tiny bit, agitated because he had no idea where he was going either. At that moment, I could feel a swell of emotion coming up through me. I asked him to pull over so I could process it and give us time to find our way. Tears started flowing from what had been a happy face only moments before. At that moment I asked myself where did that come from? Where have I felt this before? Who previously triggered this emotion that I suppressed? Then I remembered all the times that my ex-husband would flip out if I caused a missed turn due to navigating with a paper map. Back then, I'd suppress the emotion, mutter something under my breath and carry on. I'd been carrying that around for over ten years and up it came on that sunny Sunday drive in Oceanside, California. That instant connection was so liberating, and the release was so refreshing.

This came out of the blue for my husband and he hadn't even snapped at me. In my mind, I had disappointed him because I couldn't do the job I was given. I had a reaction and resolution within 5 minutes, and it was gone. Carrying the baggage of disappointing people must have come from when I was a child. I always wanted to please my parents, teachers, in fact, anyone who I interacted with. I'm a recovering people-pleaser. I remember working on this with an Energy Healer and it rooted down to wanting to be loved. Growing up, I don't remember hearing the words I love you, but I knew I was loved and looked after. So much of the baggage that we hold onto is from not knowing what it is at all. It's attached to something, somewhere within you. When you're able to tap in and find it, it's like putting down a 100-pound suitcase.

Ego loves to create its own stories when you don't know the answers. That's what your stuff is all about. You've created a story about why you need to carry something, and you won't put it down because that's not how the story goes. When you believe it long enough, it becomes a part of your subconscious and finds its own track to run on each time you encounter a similar situation. It's time to finish writing the ending of those stories that still have issues attached to them. It's not your burden to carry. Take responsibility and create the experience you want to live. I'm pretty sure it doesn't involve carrying around stuff from years and years ago. Have you heard the story of the two monks who came to a river and saw a woman in distress that needed to cross? Here it is...

A senior monk and a junior monk were traveling together. At one point, they came to a river with a strong current. As the monks were preparing to cross the river, they saw a very young and beautiful woman also attempting to cross. The young woman asked if they could help her cross to the other side.

The two monks glanced at one another because they had taken vows not to touch a woman.

Then, without a word, the older monk picked up the woman, carried her across the river, placed her gently on the other side, and carried on with his journey.

The younger monk couldn't believe what had just happened. After rejoining his companion, he was speechless, and an hour passed without a word between them.

Two more hours passed, then three, until finally the younger monk could not contain himself any longer, and blurted out,

"As monks, we are not permitted to touch a woman, how could you then carry that woman on your shoulders?"

The older monk looked at him and replied, "Brother, I set her down on the other side of the river, why are you still carrying her?"

Ask yourself how much unnecessary baggage am I carrying around because I won't put it down?

FINDING *Her*
NEXT STEPS

1. Question #7 we talked about triggers and here we are again. Those triggers are unnecessary baggage you're carrying. Having a conversation without any emotional or energetic triggers is what we all aim for. Pleasant conversations are easy. Triggering conversations are happening for a reason. Your body wants to get rid of that unnecessary baggage. Don't avoid those conversations. Make note of what's happening, who's involved, where you are, etc. These are all signals to remind you of what needs to be released.

2. Stories fill our minds. Fantasy and reality can get blurred and then Ego throws in the stories that it created. Catch yourself if you're finding your storytelling ego is filling in the blanks of something that didn't happen. When the story starts creating itself, stop it by saying "the story I'm telling myself is..." and the reality will start to dissolve. Carrying around those stories is taking up energy and room for reality.

3. Open the door to those emotions that want out. Those energy shifts are happening for a reason and your body will thank you for releasing them. Stop carrying them around. Unnecessary stuff takes up room from the wonderful stuff. Wouldn't you rather have loving, kind, happy emotions flowing freely through your body than fear, sadness, and worry?

Thoughts & Feelings

Thoughts & Feelings

Stay strong and stop yourself from winning back to what was.

QUESTION #15

What regular routine that is connected to my past do I need to release?

Did you know there are still dinosaurs roaming the earth? Not the kind you may think. The ones I'm talking about are habitual dinosaurs and you may just be one yourself. I know I am. If you've ever said "but that's the way I've always done it", then you're a habitual dinosaur. Holding on to past routines that don't fit into the present is exhausting and needs to change. Imagine the stale energy you're holding onto that needs to be released so that a fresh new approach to things can be reset. How refreshing would that be?

Transitions make us change the way things are. When you get married, you can't keep going back to your parent's house at night to go to bed. That routine needs to be released. When our children grow up, move on and start their new lives, we can't treat them like the little boy or girl that we are holding as beautiful memories in our hearts. When you learn to let go of what was, face what is and ready yourself for what will be, that step-by-step transitional approach creates the ability to release old routines rather than putting old ways in new places.

In William Bridge's book, Transitions, that I mentioned in Question #13, he talks about a man who retired and was now at home with his wife. She had established a working kitchen that was lovely and efficient. Well, one day when her husband was alone, he decided to take his skills from work and put them into play in their kitchen. He re-organized everything in the way he found efficient, and you can guess what the results were when his wife got home. He was taking his old ways and trying to apply them to a new situation. He'd been eating in the kitchen for 30 years and it never bothered him before that the pots and pans were in that drawer over there. The way he operated at work for 30 years didn't provide him with its routine any longer so, he attempted to place it in his new world with very unfavorable results.

I carried a doozy of a routine into my second marriage that was rooted in me since childhood. Growing up, we ate at 5:00pm after my Dad got home from work. My mum was a machine at routines like this. So, there I was, knowing this routine for 20 years and having applied it to my family when I had children and needed a routine. Dinner is at a set time every night. I think ours was set at 5:30pm because my ex-husband was done at work at random times. I rolled that routine into my second marriage when I was home between jobs, and set dinner for 5:30pm. My husband stopped work at 5:00pm and that gave him time to get home, barely. Some days he walked in the door, dropped his stuff and came right to the table. I didn't see anything wrong with that until it was my turn to get home, drop my stuff and head right to the table. Then I understood the meaning of downtime or transitioning between things. There was no reason to be so regulated with mealtimes. Nobody had sports or events to go rushing out the door to. We could eat whenever we wanted. It took some time for me to release that routine because that's the way it had always been for me. Insert my picture as a Habitual Dinosaur 'here'.

That scheduled dinner time was a safety control that ensures that everything will be fine. It's really a form of control, isn't it? Unnecessary routine has moments of control. It has a high attachment to the outcome, very low fluidity or flexibility and a high level of needing to be right (because that's the way I've always done it). You may be this person, or you may know someone who has a set routine in the morning. You can almost hear them saying "This is what I do, this is how I do it and nobody better mess with my routine". Even after marriage, children and other life changes, a person can still be like clockwork in their routine. Like I said earlier, this is a control mechanism for some. They're in control and they don't have to trust that someone else will do or not do for them.

What about a routine in the name of energy? Unnecessary routines that you established in your past to protect your energy are like walls that someone else needs to climb to reach you. I know people who have routines that they establish when leaving work and coming home to family. They do specific things to reset themselves and transition to a new setting. These are important to have but, when they affect the other people, it's time for a change. It's time to take responsibility for your own experiences and look past yourself and into the atmosphere you orbit in. If you're the person that stopped at the bar everyday after work for a drink when you were single but continues doing it after you have a family, look at adjusting to your new life.

The first step is the awareness that something needs to change. That's taking responsibility. If the idea of changing a routine creates anxiety, ask yourself the questions from Question #13, in The New Beginning, "Is there something I don't want to look at?" There's a reason why you're attached to that routine even though life is changing around you. Then ask yourself, "What am I willing to do to make this change happen? How much of me is going to show up?" Be intent and willing to make an effective change and release a routine that feels like a security blanket. If it causes any kind of energy shift within you, feel into it. The truth doesn't always feel good, but it feels right.

Old routines, self-limiting beliefs, and stories you hold within are all unnecessary baggage and hard to put down. Everything you hold onto takes up energy. Imagine releasing everything that no longer serves you and allowing that stale energy to leave with it. That could be the biggest, deepest breath you'll ever take. You can release those things by bringing them into your conscious mind. They're buried in your subconscious and take up unnecessary space. Do you have a closet in your home that "other stuff" goes into? Older purses that you may use someday? Books that you'll likely never read again? Household trinkets? Those are the material equivalents of your unnecessary baggage. If you were to bring all those things out of that closet and put them around your house, I bet you'd deal with them a lot quicker than keeping them in the closet. That's just like your baggage. Get it out of your subconscious. Let it be present in your conscious mind and you'll want to deal with it. Bring something forward that you know you don't want to deal with. Write it out, type it out, talk it out. Find a comfortable way for you to bring it forward. What will follow is that the energy attached to that thought, story or belief will be on the move. Let it move!! Cry, get mad, start laughing uncontrollably - whatever comes up, let it out. Repressed emotions are attached to that. You may find deeper issues attached to a routine that you can't let go of. There's likely a deeper reason why that routine is stuck on repeat. Find out what it is. Keep peeling layers, digging deep to reveal the truth. Talk to relatives who may understand things from further back. Maybe that routine you have is something you picked up from your mum, who picked it up from her dad, who got it from his mother. Find the root. That's the critical part. When you do, it'll be like a valve has been released and your attachment will be gone.

Don't let routines define who you are. Some habitual family patterns need to come to an end. Let yourself be the one that cuts the link and releases the energy that's been carried around for generations. What habitual routine, that has no purpose, can you start processing to release?

FINDING *Her*
NEXT STEPS

1. You may be in the stage of moving towards retirement or you may have someone in your life that's going through that transition. Mix routine with age and it's hard to let go of everything that's been a norm for many years. If you or someone you know is experiencing this, give it time. Even empty nesters need adjustment times. The beauty of these transitions is letting go of the way it's always been and giving yourself permission to just be. The readjustment pendulum can swing to the far left and then the far right for a while as the adjustment settles. As long as old habits are being released, the pendulum will gradually settle in the middle.

2. Is what you're holding onto a form of control or comfort? Releasing things that bring a sense of comfort isn't an easy task and doesn't need to be done unless it's interfering with what is. Maybe a replacement is needed if it's a comforting routine. If there's an energy shift whenever it happens and it causes grief or anxiety, revisit the routine. You'll know when it's time to change.

3. Growth requires change. Make a list of all the things that you know you need to release. Doesn't mean you have to release them now, but creating that list brings everything to the forefront. Remember those energy shifts. If you feel it, there's a reason for it. Stale energy attached to a routine is indicative of a stale routine. Time for some house and soul cleaning!

What did you reveal?

Listen within for the answers

that align with you.

QUESTION #16

Did this awareness come from me or someone else?

You are influenced by so much around you. What to wear, which toothbrush to buy, where to vacation or even your shade of lipstick. You look for outside influences when you're trying to find answers to the questions that you have within. You've probably spent time online trying to find out what others are saying about a similar situation you're experiencing. "How do I stop feeling stuck?" "How do I become spiritual?" "How do I find my life's purpose?"

It's human nature to look for answers to things you can't solve yourself. Scientists call it research. Research is the process of solving problems and finding facts in an organized way. That seems like a perfectly natural way to find out what your life's purpose is, right? One online search on "How do I stop feeling stuck" resulted in 139,000,000 results in .42 seconds. AWESOME! Somewhere in there is your answer, and then you'll be on your way. Maybe it's "5 things to do if you're feeling stuck in life" or "How do I find my purpose?" There are lots of great results and even some that I would suggest to anyone trying to find their path or their HERwithin. However, if it's not what your soul is looking for, or the answers your ego is searching for, they won't work for you. You'll keep searching and looking for someone to give you the answers that you think you need.

One popular form of research is "Coffee with a friend or

relative". When you find that person that you can confide in and share your stuckness with, and if you value their opinion, it's like a pot of gold. How did they do it? How long did it take? What can I change to make this go away? Ask the questions, and you'll be sure to get an answer to everything. However, if it's a spiritual life transition that you're experiencing, I can guarantee that what they say will be superficial to what you need to do. It may be equivalent to that chocolate bar at 3pm that gives you a momentary boost. Or, they may say something that triggers something within you. Remember the questions to ask yourself when you're being triggered? They were in Question #7. Find out why there's a trigger. That's a nugget of information on your journey that you must not avoid.

My experience was all of the above. I researched online, bought more than enough self-help books, looked for support and guidance from friends (who weren't going down the same rabbit hole as me, but I needed to hear other's stories to quantify mine), found some triggers, listened to countless spiritual podcasts and continued questioning myself more than ever before. All of this had one thing in common. I wasn't finding my answers. I was searching for someone or something to give me the answers. I didn't know at the time that the only one who held those answers was me. It wasn't until the very first retreat that I went on in 2016, that I found that connecting to my body again would open the door to those answers I was looking for. That door was marked HER and I was seeing glimpses of my HERwithin. I needed to become quiet and listen carefully for the guidance from within that I was craving. Did you ever have a teacher when you were very young, that spoke very quietly? Everyone gathered around on the carpet, sat quietly and listened to every word that teacher said. I believe those teachers are put on our life path to teach us how to get quiet and listen. In life, there are so many distractions and detours that take you off course. That's when you start reaching out looking for answers.

Remember the book, Are You My Mother? That little bird asked and asked if other animals and things were his mother. He didn't know what he was looking for. It wasn't until he came upon the Snort that it took him to where he needed to be. Sometimes you just need some guidance to take you to where your answers are. If you sit quietly, as the school children on the classroom carpet, the answers will come to you. Nobody else holds your answers but you. It can take time to find them and sometimes they just appear. Listen within and when an awareness arises, you'll know that it came from within and not from someone else.

When you surrender to your HERwithin and let the communication, love or guidance flow, you Allow HER to communicate with you. Let down the drawbridge, knock down that wall around your heart, take off that armour and let HER flow freely within you. She's like your heartbeat that is always there making sure you're alive to witness the new day. You're probably wondering why you haven't been hearing or feeling HER even though she's been communicating with you. There are varying degrees of awakened intuition, from beginner to pure connectedness. You have the intuitive ability built right in. Your HERwithin is your intuition. When you remove those internal barriers, you can Allow HER to communicate with you and you'll be surprised by what you're capable of. When you tune into your own awareness level, you won't be influenced by outsiders. You're at your source of everything you need to know. You're with HER. Those nudges or "out of the blue" thoughts that come to you, that's HER. Trust HER and you'll find that internal line of communication opens up and your awareness will truly come from within.

FINDING *Her*

NEXT STEPS

1. So, what you've been doing hasn't been working, right? I totally understand. I've been down that path. Your next step is to change your approach. If a plane can't land because of wind direction, they change their approach to the runway. If you have stacks of self-help books, pack them away for a few weeks to remove the research clutter from your sight. Quieten down your social media and online research for a few weeks. Change your approach and listen to the messages from within. Become vulnerable and open. Create a new routine. Meditate to calm your mind. The point is that you need to clear the pathway of all the debris so you can focus on the source of the answers. YOU!

2. This is your journey and with a bit of guidance, trust in yourself, and HER, you'll find your answers. Have conversations with yourself through journaling, voice recordings or just plain old talking to yourself. Get your own conversations going. That's where the answers are. Ask questions when you go to sleep at night and watch for the answers to appear the next day, or even in the middle of the night. The answers are there.

3. Hear HER, Feel HER, Trust HER, Follow HER, Accept HER, Understand HER, Honor HER, Respect HER, Be HER, Love HER and most of all … Find HER!

What bubbled up?

Live the life

your soul craves.

QUESTION #17

Has something gone unlived within me?

When I was 3, I was a doctor, and my patients never complained. Then I wanted to be a teacher at 6. A poet at 10. A pop star's girlfriend at 14 and a hotel front desk manager at 17. These were the stories that shaped my life. These were my dreams of my 'unstoried self'. It was me and HER creating this wondrous path that I was walking. I did eventually end up in the hospitality industry but not as a Front Desk Manager. That's a part of my unstoried self. The stories that pull us away from HER are the ones we hear, the false ones we tell ourselves and the ones decided for us. Somewhere along the way, I started to believe that I couldn't do certain things in life. Those are the stories that turn into regrets. There are many definitions of the unstoried self, but the one I came across referred to that part of you that hasn't been written yet. I don't mean literally written, like a biography, I mean the part of you that's trying to break through and ended up on the cutting room floor. What's that thing you wanted to do since you were a child but you never "got around to it"? It's still in there. If it was once a spark, you can fan that spark and turn it into the raging fire that will power you through to completion.

I love hearing about later in life reboots. Women who go back to university to get a degree after their kids are in school. I have a friend who did exactly that. She always dreamed of owning a ranch with horses of all sizes, and now she's doing that too. Vera Wang was 40 when she started in the fashion industry. Laura Ingalls Wilder, author of Little House on the Prairie books was 65 when she started writing her first successful series of books.

I always wanted to be a teacher. I loved all my school teachers, but gradually, I was enticed into the Tourism & Hospitality industry. I remember being in Europe in Grade 12 for a marching band tour and I loved meeting the people at the front desk of each hotel we stayed at. They were multi-taskers, courteous hosts and provided anything for anyone. They made people happy. In my eyes that was the perfect job for me, since I love to make people happy. After graduating high school, I got my diploma in Tourism & Hospitality then got a job as an Information Counsellor helping visitors on summer vacation. I gradually worked my way into supervisory positions including Supervisor of spectator accommodations for the 1988 Winter Olympics. Then my role shifted and I became a mum and stayed home for the next 15 years. I was just like those front desk people at the hotels. I provided everything for everyone to keep them happy but, was this what I wanted to do? I started craving a job again and returned to the tourism industry.

Within me, there was still an unstoried self. I didn't know what it was. I was moving within the industry every two years, gaining a lot of varied experience, but not finding satisfaction for too long. I took a sabbatical at one point but went right back to what I was doing with the same lingering "what else is there?" "What am I missing?" Then, in 2016 after my mum passed away at the age of 77, a little conversation about regret stuck in my mind. Mum and I didn't have very many deep conversations, but this one, a month before she passed, will live with me forever. She mentioned that she wished she would have traveled more. She was a dedicated gardener and spent months planning, growing, planting, tending and then readying the garden for the next growing season. She wished she had let the garden go for a while and went travelling with my dad or even with a group after Dad passed away. I never knew that about her. I had no idea but, here we were talking in her new room in a carefully chosen care facility and she knew for sure that this was a regret that she would take with her. Within the following month, I knew I had to dig down and find out if I was holding any regrets. I was in my early 50s at the time and I'm sure there was something. I had traveled, I had some great careers, I have an awesome family, I ... then it hit me. I've tried to work for myself three times and I gave up within the first year every time. Was that something that I needed to dig into? Did I need to give entrepreneurship everything I had, even if I felt like a failure in the past? Three months after mum passed, the word HERwithin came to me and I knew I needed to share what I had just discovered so that other women could start living that life they're craving.

Even while writing this book, I'm still molding and creating HERwithin after three years. I made it past the 1 year drop off zone. I noticed something different though. As HERwithin evolves, so do I. I've transitioned, peeled, awakened and found HER within me, and I have a personal connection to HERwithin. I can't shelve it and go work for someone else. There have been days of tears and "I can't do this any longer", and then I get a sign from the universe.

One day I was waiting for a medical appointment at a hospital when a gurney and two EMS people went past me. On that gurney was an elderly lady with her face scraped up, a neck brace on and one of the EMS persons was holding her hand. My heart sank when I saw her go by. Ten minutes later, they came past in the other direction. This time a young lady was holding her hand while the EMS people followed. As the gurney went past me, that beautiful elderly lady said, "I'm glad I got my hair done this morning". I felt like my heart grew ten times its size at that moment. It's all about perspective. There I was, feeling like I needed to walk away from something, and not live out my unstoried self. Yet I needed to look at the good in my life. Like being grateful for my new hairdo after being struck by a car.

I've always wanted to be a teacher, and here I am. I'm mentoring women on how to navigate mid-life so they can live the life they want instead of the one they think they should have. My unstoried self is shrinking as my storied self grows. I'm speaking, writing, teaching and changing lives daily. When you stay curious, a nudge from within just might become your new path. It may be that unstoried self from years ago that found an opening to re-introduce itself. Take time to look within and journal out those secrets that you're holding close to your heart. So many people before you have taken that scary step forward. I've learned to trust, forgive, set boundaries, respect the process and love myself. As international best-selling author, speaker and research professor Brené Brown is quoted, "if I'm not going to try and change it, then who?"

Be the one. Don't wait until you're being cared for to live your unstoried self. Care for yourself now! Has something gone unlived in you?

FINDING *Her*
NEXT STEPS

1. A regret that's held onto and not fulfilled is like standing in a jail cell holding the key yelling to be let out. You hold the key to what you do or don't do. It doesn't matter if you're 50, 60 or 70, give it a try and then put it down. Don't carry around those things that have gone unlived in your life. Even if you try it a little bit so you can say you did, you're taking a step away from being unlived into a place of living. Make a list of the things you want to try and move it forward into your conscious and out of the subconscious.

2. Is it really unlived? Are you putting a label on something or putting restrictions on something you're afraid to do? I wanted to be a teacher and now I realize I'm teaching. It's not in a school setting or a lecture hall, but I teach women every day. What is it you want to try that you can do your own way? Want to be a welder? Take a course. Want to write a book? Start typing. Sometimes it's one step that's stopping the beginning. You don't need to see every step on the staircase to know it reaches the top.

3. There's a conversation in your head that's stopping you. Write down the narrative of that conversation and the people involved. Is it true?

Thoughts & Feelings

Thoughts & Feelings

Keep your energy moving
like a flowing river.
Don't dam it up.

QUESTION #18

Do I allow myself space for things to move through me?

If you're like me, and many other women, you probably don't make time to reset your opinions about spirituality and self-care and let things naturally move through you. Right? You have things to do, places to be and internal conversations to avoid. Who has time for this mind, body and soul to start processing differently? A very legitimate question that I had before my intense transition when I had an emotional, spiritual, mental and physical multi car pile up on my life's purpose highway. I suppressed everything until I basically exploded inside.

I had such a chokehold on life because I didn't trust what was happening to me or around me. Then my body decided to inform me of my poor decision-making skills by creating something that nobody could find an answer to. Have you ever gone for an ultrasound, x-ray or blood test and heard that everything was in optimal condition? Then what was causing this pain? Remember back in Question #8 when you asked yourself if you are aware of the energetic shifts in your body? Remember EMOTION = Energy in Motion? That's something I didn't know back then. I was powering through my days trying to avoid dealing with whatever was wanting out. "I can't be weak. I must be strong." "Suppress! Suppress! Suppress!" "Nobody can see me cry." But that's what I needed to do. Instead, I became angry and stuck in a pattern of control. I wasn't creating the anger; it was swirling around within me looking for a way out. My confusion with life and just being me had started to fester and turn into something ugly.

Along with the anger came severe gut issues and more tests. The emotional, mental and physical blocks that I had put up were being brought to my attention from within, but I wouldn't listen to them. I could fix this with another kind of medication from my many doctors. I wish I knew then what I know now.

To allow yourself space for energy to move through you is one of the most beautiful forms of self-care you will ever experience. You are a soul in a human body. This container of flesh, bones and organs is the vessel that takes your soul through life. When you don't allow your soul to do its work, you start damaging the vessel you live in. Imagine piloting a boat that is designed beautifully to ride in the open waters. It floats across the waves and brings such a feeling of peace. When you take that same vessel and try to float it down a river, it's going to get damaged but hey, it's a ship, this is water, it should just do what it's supposed to do. You're forcing it to do what it's not meant for. Much like you. When you force your body to suppress the energy that it needs to expel, you cause damage to your vessel. Lesson learned and now the repairs are underway.

I think back on all the things that I would complain about, and I think how easy it would have been to face the energy that needed to be moved. I had knee issues growing up. I thought it was hereditary. My grandpa had a knee replacement so I thought it must be the same thing. Now I know it's not. I have become a student of understanding the connection between the mind, body and soul. By reading and understanding the connection within, I've had the opportunity to heal myself from smaller ailments like sore ankles, shoulders or neck that come out of the blue. We hold emotions and trauma at a cellular level in our body. Those emotions and trauma are trapped negative energy that need to be released. When we're faced with a situation that creates an energetic shift in our body, followed by pain or discomfort, that's your body's signal to you that something needs to be released. Authors like Louise Hay, Carolyn Myss and Dr Michael Lincoln all have books on the connection of the body, mind and soul along with tools to help release that trapped energy.

One day, I announced that I was going to run an eight-week group coaching program. I felt good about it, and I was full of high energy. I created a great format for the program and I announced it to my tribe on social media. That was about 3pm on a Monday. Later that evening I started getting a pain behind my right ear. It wasn't in my ear; it was behind my ear on my neck. I thought it was from sitting at my computer typing for too long so, what did I do, I took a muscle relaxant. Remember, I can fix anything with another drug! I went to bed that night and woke up with the sensation that I was under water. I couldn't hear properly. That's when I turned to my information on the body, mind and soul connection. I know that there's a connection to the ears, nose and throat because of previous surgeries, so my approach was to do some research on energy in that area. Blocked ears/hearing is an energetic response to the fear of hearing something. Was I afraid to hear what people would say about my program? Was I afraid of rejection? What was I afraid of? Even though I had the energetic surge to create and announce the program, my ego had enough time overnight to taint that energy and have it manifest as an ear condition. Energetic suppression or resurgence doesn't need a lot of time to manifest. Normally, I would have gone to the doctor and had them deal with it. Not any longer. When I go to bed feeling healthy and wake up not healthy, I know I'm experiencing an energetic shift that needs to be faced right away.

I chose to do a throat chakra meditation. I gathered every blue crystal I owned because blue is the color aligned with the throat chakra, put ylang ylang essential oil in a diffuser and on a necklace, then with a message to my beautiful energy goddess Charlotte, I found the root. It wasn't until the evening that I got my instructions from Charlotte. She sent me a paragraph from an amazing book that she uses called Messages from the body by Michael J. Lincoln Ph.D. (I now own the book). Her text message basically said that 'I had been hurt by nasty words in the past and my subconscious had brought that forward as a reminder that if I put myself out there, it will happen again. This pattern was established around the time I was 24 years old and I held onto it'. For the life of me, I couldn't find the incident that caused it, so Charlotte suggested that I go somewhere quiet and just read the passage. I did, and within five seconds, I was in tears in my office. I sat in the dark and let the tears flow because I was finally giving myself the space to let this thing move through me.

Unknowingly, you hear things as an adult and suppress them or you think you let them go. Chances are, much like me, there's something within you that is waiting to be released from your past and find a way out. You may face this type of thing over and over in your life and keep suppressing or trying to ignore it. It's when you give it the space to move, that this energy finally starts to clear. It can be in the form of tears, anger or even hysterical laughter. Whatever it is, it needs out. Your subconscious will label things for you that you can't find a name for. Before my sister was born, my parents had a hyper-focus on me due to allergies and serious eczema. Anything would trigger a flare-up, and I was continuously watched when it came to food, new clothes, environment and animals. Nevertheless, when my sister was born, my ego decided to tell me that I wasn't important anymore because there was a baby now, and mum and dad were no longer focused on me. I didn't tell myself that in so many words, after all, I was five years old, but I held that belief in my subconscious for fifty years. Now I look back and see myself feeling small in so many situations. I never allowed myself to be fully me and carried around imposter syndrome when I did do something remarkable. My ear thing, that was imposter syndrome.

That night when I went to bed, I could feel a lighter version of me floating around me. I had released something from my past just by reading the passage that Charlotte had sent me. I don't question the how's and why's and what's any longer. I just accept that that's what needed to be done. Before I contacted Charlotte, I did a meditation, on my own, holding all my blue crystals, and witnessed a veil being pulled off me. It was a shroud of something that I was releasing. I had a chakra clearing done not long before this all happened. I believe that the combination of that previous clearing and throat chakra energy clearing I did was strong enough to help my soul remove a strong false limiting belief about myself. As I said, I don't know how or why this happened at that time, but it was time. By removing that veil, my creative energy jumped into overdrive, my confidence in what I do feels fresh, authentic and incredible. My decisions are focused and strong. My internal drive is pure and I'm not hiding behind a mask of imposter syndrome any longer. How do I know that? I'm writing a book!

Next time you feel something shift, or you know something is off, give yourself the space to let it move through you. Sit quietly and don't think, just feel. What are you feeling? Imagine that it's coming up through your body and out through your eyes or fingertips. What does that energy or emotion need to do? What are you telling yourself and is it true? Keep the energy moving within you like a beautiful flowing river. Don't let your emotions dam it up. Surrender and let it flow.

FINDING *Her*
NEXT STEPS

1. Face your fears! How long have you been avoiding something? Avoiding reality is like constantly being chased. Stop running. It's ok to feel your way through something. Yes, it's scary and yes, you need to be vulnerable. If you take the time, in a private space, to open those doors, you'll feel better for it.

2. Journal your ailments. I know this sounds like you're focusing on the negative, but if you are aware that your back goes out after a specific encounter, you'll start to see patterns. Everything from a blister to the flu has emotional energy attached to it. For one week, make a record of every message that your body is sending you. A situation that's happening when it appears is reminding you of an initial incident where you buried your emotions. That energy needs out.

3. Trust yourself during this process. Your initial reaction will be denial. It happened to me until I started seeing results. Your ego will do everything it can to keep things from changing. Trust HER and the response to that message from your body. Allow emotion to bubble up. Trust me, this is a giant rabbit hole and once you make the connection, you'll wonder why you didn't do it earlier. Find a trusted friend that you can process with. Talking things through out loud help to process and bring up those emotions that need to be released.

What did you reveal?

What did you reveal?

When your soul speaks to
you, it speaks from love.

QUESTION #19

Who am I without my titles?

I remember sitting at a patio table having coffee with a girlfriend, and I asked her "how would you answer the question, who am I?" She said, "That's easy, I'm a woman, wife, mother, successful businesswoman, I'm a sister, a daughter, grandma, gardener and avid wine drinker." I was impressed with the list that she came up with so quickly, but then I asked her another question. She readied herself and I asked, "Who are you without all those titles?" I wish I could have captured all the facial expressions she went through trying to find her answer. It was like all the answers she gave me were now being wiped from her consciousness and there was nothing there to replace them. She looked at me with a furrowed brow and said, "I don't know. Who am I?"

The question I asked wasn't "what" are you. That's an easy thing for anyone to describe because 'what' is tangible. It's an object or a thing. Like a wine drinker or a grandma. There's a security in calling yourself something because it's not attached to the deeper personal side of your soul. It takes vulnerability to expose that space and be confident with your answers. So, my girlfriend asked me the same question, and I couldn't answer it. It's fine and dandy to do all this research and ask people the questions but, I needed to find my own answers. Knowing who I was would be a guiding light to get others thinking about who they are.

One day, I decided to write everything about myself on a whiteboard. I started with the obvious of what I am. I couldn't stop writing. I am a mum, stepmom, wife, ex-wife, aunt, sister, daughter, niece, friend, confidant, manager, co-worker, gardener, cook and the list went on and on. That was easy but, that's not what I was looking for. The next batch of descriptors I wrote was like something you'd find on my resume. I am ... curious, motivated, organized, efficient, focused, balanced and again, not what I knew I needed to write out. It was like I was hiding from being exposed as something I'm not. Maybe it's something I want to be but I'm not living up to it. Or, was it the imposter syndrome rearing its ugly head and telling me that I'm not who I think I am? Where was I going to find these beautiful, special words that I wanted to hear about myself? Was it because I'd never heard them before that I didn't know what I was searching for? I remember my older brother telling me that it doesn't matter what others think of you. That's none of your business. I was looking for something that other people saw in me. I could start asking everyone what they thought, but I had to step out from behind my ego, show myself my vulnerability and be honest with myself.

This exercise in Who Am I created so many questions, and it was also the point in time that I realized I had so many questions that are going unanswered. I looked everywhere, I did every quiz I could find, read more self-help books and even started asking my friends. In Question #17, remember when I asked Did this awareness come from within or was it someone else's suggestion? Well, I didn't know what I was looking for and whatever I heard sounded just perfect. The beautiful thing about asking people "who you are" is that they will probably tell you all the lovely things that they see in you. Remember, that's what they see. These are their answers, through their filters. It's also a reflection of themselves. If they don't possess what you have, they won't see it in you. Don't doubt your answers from within because "When you look beyond yourself, for the answers that already lay within, you dismiss your own wisdom". – Janis Doherty

Now it was time to step back from all the outside influences I had reached out to and put away everything I heard. It was time for me to figure out who I am without my titles. It didn't matter how perfect my desk was or what tea I was drinking, this was uncomfortable. I fidgeted and squirreled off by cleaning stuff up or surfing social media. I even searched online for "how do I describe who I am" and again, those were the resume descriptors that I had no problem creating. Why was this so hard? When I first tried this, I didn't have the grasp on meditation like I have today. I am now far more grounded and understand my messages that come from within.

I'm going to close my eyes, while I sit here typing, and see what comes to me today. We change and reveal parts of ourselves regularly, especially when we do the deep inner work and peel away life layers that no longer serve us. Get comfortable and say I AM and receive what comes to you. Here you go; I AM...

Pure, Energy, HER (that one brought up tears), Beauty, Able, Free, Harmonious, My Spirit

That took me 2 minutes because I'm so quickly grounded and connected to my HERwithin and I feel the words come through me. That's probably why I got tears when HER came up. I've been working for years to make that connection as beautiful and true as I can. She came through with flying colors today. I just had another one trickle through, and it said "unmasked". These are my answers that came directly from my soul. When your soul speaks to you, it speaks with love. There's no judgement and it's truly who you are. Anything that comes to you that's not dripping with love isn't from your soul. Be careful not to interpret the answers from your ego as your Who Am I answers. Answers that come from ego are judgemental and questioning. When your soul is speaking to you, that's the truth. That's where you started from and it knows who you are. All the life layers that have clouded your view and created a disconnect has you doubting that you are what you hear from within.

Think of the last funeral you were at. How did the people giving eulogies talk about the dearly departed? They talk about their titles and cover all their accomplishments throughout their lifetime. You will always hear something like, "she was kind, compassionate, giving, empowering, free, rich with love and a beautiful soul". That's a beautiful description of who that person was. Don't wait for someone to describe you in your eulogy. Find those answers within yourself. Remove your armour and stand naked in your wholeness and feel the energy of who you are. That isn't something that was even remotely easy for me to consider pre-transition. I had titles, but I needed to rediscover who I am.

Update: Nine months after writing this chapter, I was in the editing stage, and as I was reading my list, I had a flood of new ones. Being a breast cancer survivor, I have opened up a secret room of emotions and sensations. Within that room was I AM grateful, vulnerable, honest, humorous, receptive, forgiving, kind and spirited.

Take time to write down your words that come from within. The following journal pages are there for you to capture the spirit and energy that is flowing through you right now. Don't wait to do it later. Grab a pen and start writing whatever comes from HER. You may find emotion attached to some of your words. Don't deny the tears or giggles, or whatever comes with them. You are worthy of every beautiful word that comes from HER.

FINDING *Her*
NEXT STEPS

1. Before you go to the journal pages, you may want to take a few minutes to get the titles and corporate descriptors out of your head. As you're just starting your journey to Find HER, the thoughts and feelings that you've carried around for years can make for a cloudy connection. Grab a different piece of paper, write them all down then destroy it. The action of removing those is powerful. Now you've cleared the way to start your Who Am I journaling

2. For some deeper connection while you make your list, follow this little grounding exercise to help make a heart connection with yourself:

- Find a private setting so you can be fully immersed in this moment.

- Get comfortable and relax your forehead, then your jaw and then your shoulders.

- Place your non writing hand on your heart/heart centre and feel the connection.

- Gently say to yourself "I am..." and feel the messages coming from within.

- Emotions will bubble up so please let them flow. Don't be embarrassed.

3. Be honest. Be vulnerable. Be open. Be free. Turn off the judgement committee in your head and allow yourself to write down everything. Scribble, doodle, do whatever it takes to get the words out that you probably haven't heard yourself say before. Allow yourself to release. This doesn't have to be perfect or complete. Once you allow yourself this space, you'll find words will pop up out of the blue. I had them pop up in the shower, while driving and even while I'm going to sleep. Once your HERwithin knows the door is always open, she'll be popping by regularly. Check in with your list periodically and add whenever you want. It's a great way to give yourself a reminder of how beautiful your soul really is.

What bubbled up?

Find HER and find your BEAUTY,

JOY & SUCCESS within.

It's all HER within.

QUESTION #20

Who is that in the mirror?

Do you remember the wave that rolled through social media about the Ten-Year Gap? This was the one where you posted a picture of yourself from ten years ago and a current one. Some people enjoyed it; some people saw it as demeaning while others didn't really understand the whole reason behind it. I was one of those in the resistance party to start with. What a silly thing to do. There's no way I was going to participate in this. What was going on that made this so difficult for me? After looking at a picture of me from 2009, it hit me. I was standing, at that time, in the doorway of divorce and the memories of 2009 were not something I wanted to resurrect. As I sat looking at my picture, I remember taking that picture. I was putting together an online profile. My ex-husband had moved out of our family home; I was trying to figure out life, and the one thing I was longing for was male companionship. I wanted to be admired and to feel special. I now know that wasn't what I needed at the time, but I didn't want to deny myself those moments of feeling like a beautiful woman again.

As I contemplated even further, I realized that the smile, shining back at me from the picture, was fake. My hair color was fake. The happy person I was attempting to portray, passed as happy... but only on the outside. Inside was a different story. The more I looked at that picture, the more I wanted to delete it. Then I pulled up my picture from 10 years later. I had some professional headshots done and I had an excellent selection to pick from. The sultry, the serious, the joyous, the wise one, the cute one and the one I used. It's the most candid of the twelve that I had. It's not one I use on my website or in anything else I created because it's too … me! That's the thought that went through my mind. What better time to use it than in this challenge?

I put the two images side by side and smiled, then cried. Look at me. I'm authentic. That smile is me. That hair isn't colored any longer and I'm openly grey. The light in my eyes is me. Then I started to tear up. It's me. I have journeyed back to HER, wrapped my arms around HER and now we are one. We're harmoniously together again. Then an incredible feeling of joy encompassed my body. I have completed what I set out to do. I'm not looking for HER any longer. I am harmoniously intertwined with HER. Like a vine wrapping itself around a beautiful tree. The vine uses the tree for support and growth. The tree and the vine are meant to be together. Take away the tree, and the vine will fall to the ground with no support system. Take away the vine and the tree is bare. I'm the vine firmly wrapped around HER, the solid, beautiful oak tree. She supports me, guides me and protects me as we grow together.

To me, this challenge isn't about what I look like ten years later. It's about the growth and journey I've been on for the past ten years. I am disembarking from that ship, unpacking whatever I don't need and planning my next journey as I write this. I've found my BEAUTYwithin, CHILDwithin, SUCCESSwithin, JOYwithin and my HARMONYwithin and it's all HERwithin. All of this was being held in safekeeping by HER. She knew I'd be back, and I'd be looking for all those things I left behind.

I heard a story on a podcast the other day about a woman who went to heaven and was asked to follow an angel to these huge doors. "What's behind there?" "You'll see", said the angel. As the angel opened the doors, sparkles and bling and stacks and stacks of beautifully wrapped presents came into the light. As the woman stood speechless, the angel walked her into the room. "Do you want to know what all this is?", asked the angel. The lady replied, "This is beautiful, who is all this for?" The angel took the lady by the hand and gently said, "These are all the gifts you didn't ask for."

When I hear a story like that, I have childlike tingles of excitement. All you have to do is ask, trust and you'll receive in so many ways. I ask for guidance and help regularly when I can't find the way myself. When I go to bed in tears because I don't know what to do, I ask, and then I wake up feeling hopeful and things start to happen. I ask for my gifts now. I ask for the life that I want to live and the destiny I want to achieve. It never hurts to ask, right? That girl in the mirror ten years ago never asked for anything because she thought she didn't deserve it.

Facing my ten years ago self and looking at her resilience, courage, self-love, determination, and what looked like happiness, I now see what pieces of me were missing. I was living a must-do/must fix life, and it put me in more masculine energy than feminine energy. I was losing my nurturing side, and everything was becoming mechanical. I was controlling and it was being disguised as being efficient and organized. That's what I see in my picture from ten years ago. Now, when I look in the mirror, I see someone who trusts and is working every day to become a better version of HERself. I'll ask myself these questions in a few more years and I hope my answers and experiences are different.

FINDING *Her*
NEXT STEPS

1. Find pictures that are from ten years ago and journal what you feel when you look back. If you were in a transition, process whatever emotions come up. Take a moment and really look at yourself in the mirror. Look past your reflection and deep into your eyes. That's the beauty that others see and the beauty that's within your soul.

2. What were you covering up in the past? Have you removed the masks that stop yourself from being vulnerable and free? Anything that feels like you have to adjust yourself to fit in, is a mask that you're wearing. Look for the truth in your relationships, actions and conversations.

3. As you transition through life, take the time to ask yourself these pivotal questions over and over again because as you grow, you truly discover the woman within.

Thoughts & Feelings

THE END

or is this the beginning?

FIND *Her*   TRUST *Her*   LOVE *Her*